W9-AHG-837

W9-AHG-837

THE BIG BOOK OF
STARS & PLANETS

ROBIN KERROD

GALLERY BOOKS
An Imprint of W. H. Smith Publishers Inc.
112 Madison Avenue
New York City 10016

First published in the United States in 1990 by Gallery Books,
an imprint of W.H. Smith Publishers, Inc.,
112 Madison Avenue, New York, New York 10016

By arrangement with The Octopus Publishing Group Limited,
Michelin House, 81 Fulham Road, London SW3 6RB

Copyright © 1990 The Octopus Publishing Group Limited

All rights reserved. No part of this publication may be reproduced,
stored in a retrieval system, or transmitted, in any form or by any
means, electronic, mechanical, photocopying, recording or otherwise,
without the prior permission of The Octopus Publishing Group Limited.

ISBN 0-8317-0861-1

Printed in Great Britain by BPCC Paulton Books Ltd

Gallery Books are available for bulk purchase for sales promotions and
premium use. For details write or telephone the Manager of Special
Sales, W.H. Smith Publishers, Inc., 112 Madison Avenue, New York,
New York 10016. (212) 532-6600

CONTENTS

UNDERSTANDING THE UNIVERSE

The Universe   4
The Scale of Space   6
The Heavenly Sphere   8

THE STARS

Constellations   10
How it all Began   12
Star Rays   14
Telescopes   16
Measuring Stars   18
Star Brightness   20
Companions   22
Nebulae   24
Star Birth   26
Star Death   28
Death of the Sun   30

THE GALAXIES

Galaxies   32
Galaxy Families   34
Irregular Galaxies   36
Radio Galaxies   38

THE SUN

Our Star, the Sun   40
The Solar Wind   42
Eclipses   44
Total Eclipse   46

THE MOON

Our Neighbor, the Moon   48
Phases of the Moon   50
Lunar Odyssey   52
The Lunar Surface   54

THE PLANETS

The Planets   56
Meteors and Comets   58
Mercury and Venus   60
Planet Earth   62
Mars   64
Jupiter   66
Saturn   68
Uranus   70
Neptune and Pluto   72

EXPLORING SPACE

Space Voyagers   74
Other Worlds   76

Index   78
Acknowledgments   80

THE UNIVERSE

Astronomers use powerful telescopes on the ground and in space to try to understand the mysteries of the universe. But even through binoculars we can find out a great deal.

On every clear night of the year, nature presents one of her great spectacles – the starry heavens. On some nights, we can see a particularly brightly shining "star," which rises before the rest; we call it "the evening star." But it is not a star. It is a near neighbor in space, the planet Venus. On many nights, the Moon lightens our darkness with its silvery beams. From time to time, fiery streaks appear in the sky. These

are meteors and they look like falling stars. Comets sometimes appear and grow a tail that can reach halfway across the sky.

Stars and space, planets and moons, falling stars and comets – they all form part of what we call the universe. Everything that exists belongs to the universe.

Astronomy is the science that studies the stars and the other bodies that exist in space, and astronomers

are the scientists who practice it. Astronomers not only observe what happens in the heavens, they also try to explain what they see. They try to find out what makes the universe work.

Astronomers investigate the universe not only with their eyes, but with all kinds of powerful telescopes and instruments. They even send their instruments into space so they can see the heavens more clearly.

THE SCALE OF SPACE

When we look up into the heavens, we are looking out into space. Space looks, and is, vast. But just how big is it? The simple answer is that it is bigger than anyone can possibly imagine.

On Earth we measure distances between places in miles or kilometers. For measuring distances in space, however, these units are useless. Even the nearest star in the sky lies over 25 million million miles away! And that is only a small step in space.

To make things simpler, astronomers think about distances in space in a different way. They think in terms of how long it takes the light from a star to reach us. Light travels at a tremendous speed – some 186,000 miles per second.

The light from the nearest star, called Proxima Centauri, takes about 4¼ years to reach us. Astronomers say it lies 4¼ light-years away. They are using as a unit the light-year, which is the distance light from a star travels in a year.

To get an idea of the vastness of space, let us make an imaginary journey into the universe in a super spaceship, which can travel as fast as light. We reach the Moon in less than 1½ seconds and the Sun in 8½ minutes. After about 5 hours, we leave the solar system behind. Now comes a 4¼-year cruise through empty space before we get to the nearest stars.

If we navigated well, we could leave behind the stars in our Galaxy after about 2,000 years, then we could journey to the nearest outer galaxy. That would take 170,000 years. If we were really adventurous and wanted to go to the very edge of the universe, it would take no less than 15,000 million years. That is how vast the universe is!

Solar System

Earth

Above: With a diameter of 7,926 miles, the Earth seems big to us. But it is really only a minute speck in the universe. The diagrams show how the Earth fits into the universe as a whole: it is part of the solar system, which is part of a galaxy, and many galaxies make up the universe. We call the Sun, with its family of planets, satellites and so on, the solar system. It measures about 9,000 million miles from one side to the other.

Below: The Sun travels through space as part of a huge family, or galaxy, of other stars. The closest star to the Sun is over 25 million million miles away. Its light takes over 4 years to reach us. But light takes over 100,000 years to travel from one side of the galaxy to the other. Even this galaxy occupies only a tiny part of space. There are many millions more galaxies like it in the universe.

Universe

Galaxy

Right: In the Middle Ages people believed the Earth was the center of the universe and all the other heavenly bodies revolved around it. This picture from the 1300s shows two angels working cranks to keep the stars circling around the Earth.

THE HEAVENLY SPHERE

People first began stargazing in earnest about 5,000 years ago. That was when the first great civilizations developed in the part of the world we now call the Middle East. They included Chaldea, Babylonia, and Egypt.

It was the priests who studied the stars as they tried to find meanings in the events that took place in the heavens. They thought that the heavens ruled people's lives. We call that kind of study astrology. Many people today still believe that their lives are affected by "their stars," and read horoscopes in newspapers, but there is no evidence this is true.

What did the early priest-astrologer-astronomers think the universe was like? They decided, of course, that the Earth was the center of the universe, and that it was flat. The stars were fixed to the inside of the bowl of the heavens, which spun around Earth.

Much later, Greek philosophers such as Aristotle (4th century B.C.) suggested that the Earth was round. The stars, they said, were fixed to the inside of a great celestial (heavenly)

Below: The stars appear to whirl around the Earth. It is as though they are stuck to the inside of a great rotating sphere, with the Earth fixed at the center.

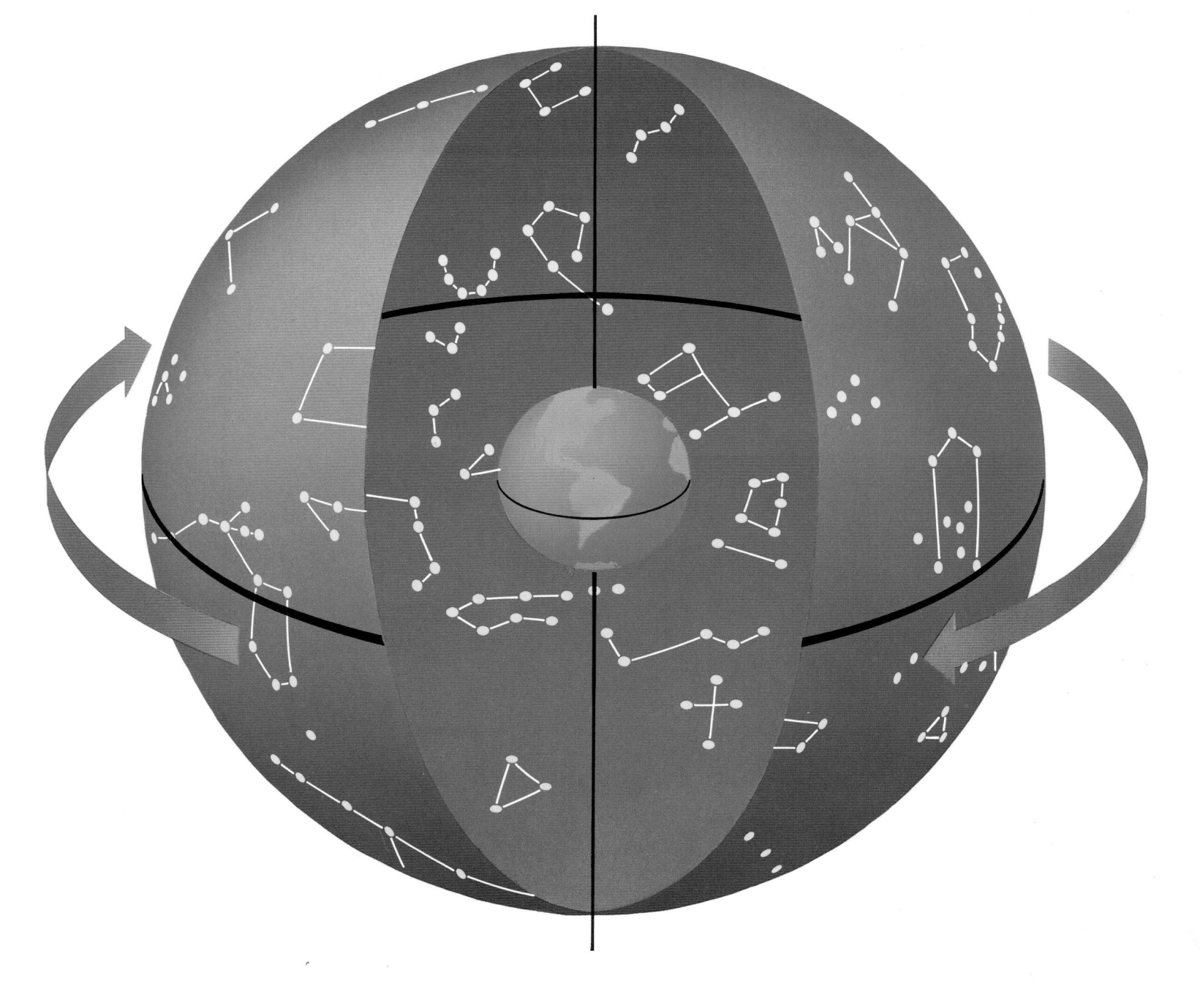

sphere, which rotated around the Earth.

Astronomers today know differently. But, nevertheless, they find the idea of a celestial sphere very useful. It provides a convenient way of pinpointing the positions of the stars in the heavens.

The Earth spins on its axis once a day. This is what makes the celestial sphere appear to rotate around it. The stars move in great circles in the heavens as the celestial sphere appears to rotate. Like the Sun, they rise in the east and set in the west.

Right: Some aspects of the celestial sphere. The ecliptic marks the Sun's path across the sphere. A star is pinpointed by its celestial latitude and longitude, called declination and right ascension.

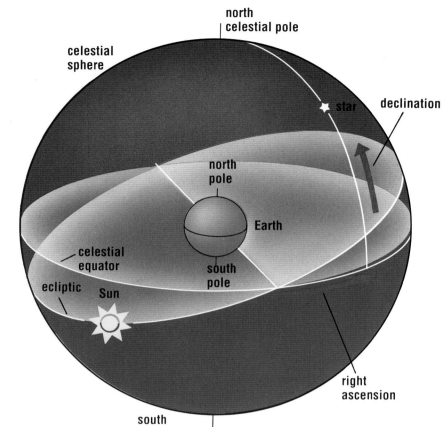

Left: When you point a camera at the Pole star, this is the kind of photograph you get. The Pole star appears as a point of light, and the other stars make circular trails around it. This happens because the Pole star lies almost directly above the Earth's axis and appears fixed. The other stars, which are away from the axis, move in circles as the celestial sphere rotates.

CONSTELLATIONS

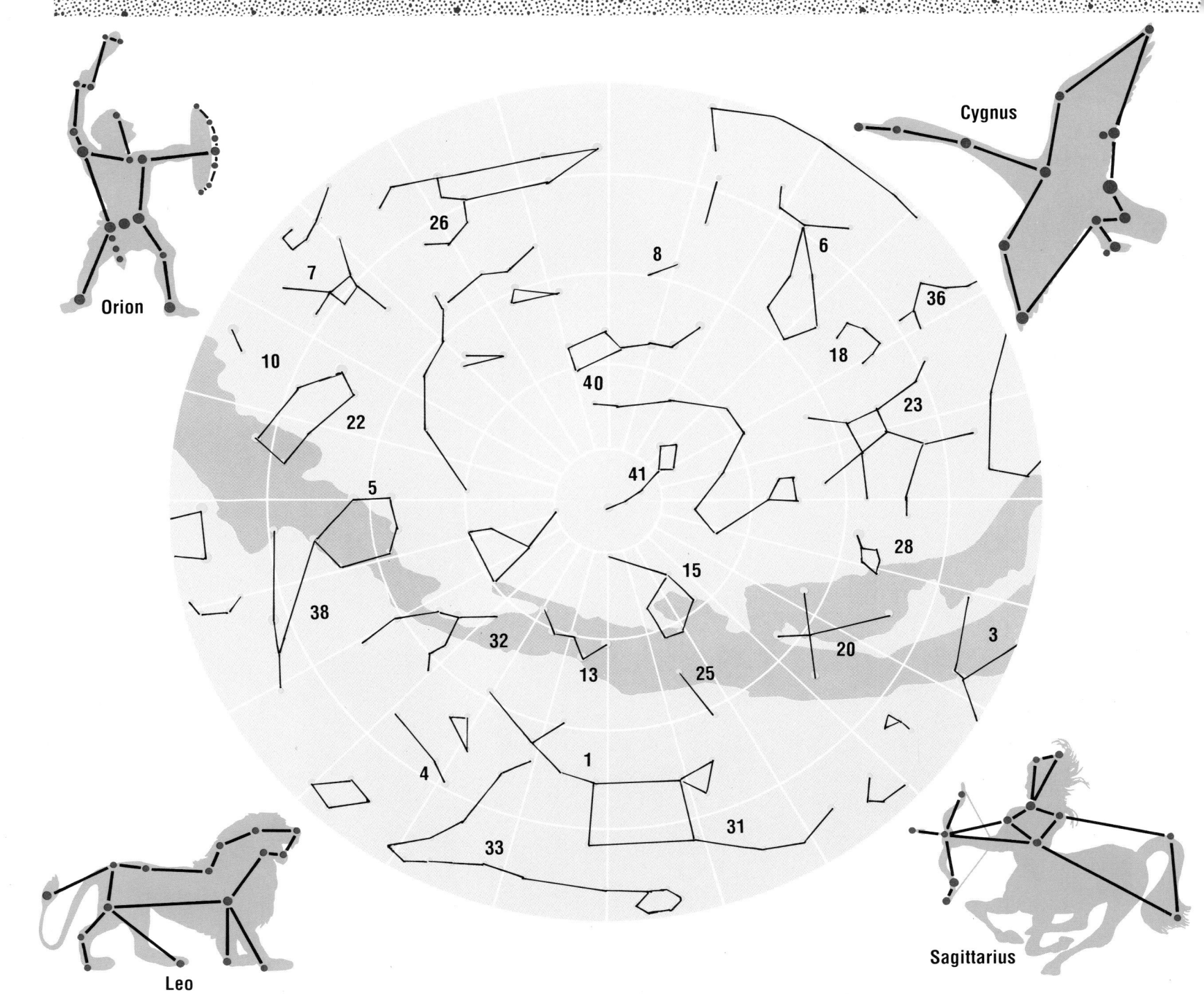

Orion

Cygnus

Leo

Sagittarius

The main star patterns, or constellations that can be seen in the skies of the Northern Hemisphere (**above**) and the Southern Hemisphere (**opposite**). The white bands mark the position of the Milky Way. The celestial poles are located in the center of each circle. Only the Northern Hemisphere has a Pole star, Polaris.

The positions of the stars in the sky change all the time because the Earth is rotating. But the positions of the stars in relation to one another appear to stay the same. The stars seem to be fixed to the sphere, as the ancients believed. Astronomers now know this is not true. The stars are moving very rapidly through space. But they are so far away that we cannot detect their movement, even after many years.

When you first gaze at the night sky, the stars appear to be dotted about haphazardly. But if you gaze for long enough, you can start to pick out patterns made by the brightest stars. We call these patterns constellations.

The constellations remain the same year in, year out. They are useful signposts for guiding us around the heavens. The early priest-astronomers of the Middle East saw almost identical constellations thousands of years ago. And they named them after figures they thought the star patterns resembled: perhaps a bear or a lion, or mythological people such as Hercules.

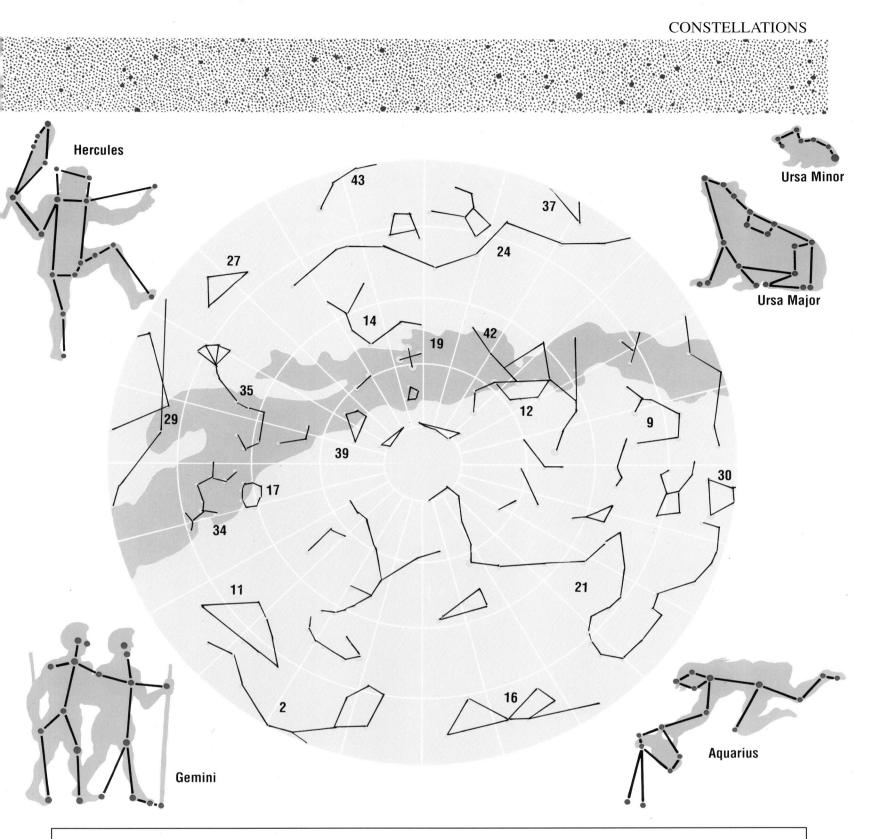

Hercules

Ursa Minor

Ursa Major

Gemini

Aquarius

MAJOR CONSTELLATIONS

	Latin name	English name		Latin name	English name		Latin name	English name
1	Andromeda	The Andromeda	16	Cetus	Whale	31	Pegasus	Winged Horse
2	Aquarius	Water Carrier	17	Corona Australis	Southern Crown	32	Perseus	Perseus
3	Aquila	Eagle	18	Corona Borealis	Northern Crown	33	Pisces	Fishes
4	Aries	Ram	19	Crux	Southern Cross	34	Sagittarius	Archer
5	Auriga	Charioteer	20	Cygnus	Swan	35	Scorpius	Scorpion
6	Boötes	Herdsman	21	Eridanus	Eridanus, The River Po	36	Serpens	Serpent
7	Cancer	Crab	22	Gemini	Twins	37	Sextans	Sextant
8	Canes Venatici	Hunting Dogs	23	Hercules	Hercules	38	Taurus	Bull
9	Canis Major	Larger Dog	24	Hydra	Water Monster	39	Triangulum	Triangle
10	Canis Minor	Lesser Dog	25	Lacerta	Lizard	40	Ursa Major	Big Dipper or Larger Bear
11	Capricornus	Horned Goat	26	Leo	Lion			
12	Carina	Keel (of a ship)	27	Libra	Scales	41	Ursa Minor	Little Dipper or Smaller Bear
13	Cassiopeia	Cassiopeia, Lady in a Chair	28	Lyra	Lyre			
14	Centaurus	Centaur	29	Ophiuchus	Water Holder	42	Vela	Sail
15	Cepheus	Cepheus, The Monarch	30	Orion	Orion, The Hunter	43	Virgo	Virgin

HOW IT ALL BEGAN

The astronomers and philosophers of the ancient world had little idea about what the universe was really like, and even less idea about how it came into being. They could only offer supernatural explanations.

The Bible explains that it was God who created Heaven and Earth, and all the creatures therein. In the 17th century, one archbishop calculated a date for the Creation. He decided it occurred on the morning of October 23, 4004 B.C.!

Even astronomers could really only make guesses about the origin of the universe until the 1920s. That was when the astronomer Edwin Hubble carried out the first comprehensive study of the outer galaxies. He discovered that they were all rushing away from us, and each other. It appeared as if the whole universe was expanding.

Hubble's work has since been confirmed many times. The universe is expanding, as if from a gigantic explosion that took place millions and millions of years ago. All astronomers now believe there was such an explosion and it created the universe.

Before about 15,000 million years ago nothing existed. There was no matter, no energy, no space. Then the universe was created in a fantastic, incredibly high temperature explosion we call the Big Bang (**below left**). And it began to expand rapidly, cooling all the while. As it cooled, clouds of matter came together under gravity to form denser and denser clouds (**below**). From these clouds the stars and galaxies were born. The universe today (**right**) is mainly empty space, with galaxies scattered here and there. It is still expanding.

Right: A shower of particles produced in a nuclear physics experiment. Astronomers think that particles like this were formed when the universe was only a few minutes old. Later, the particles began to join together to form atoms, the building blocks from which all matter is made up. The first atoms formed were of hydrogen, which became the "fuel" for the nuclear reactions that release energy to set the stars shining.

They call the explosion the Big Bang and believe it took place about 15,000 million years ago. Before then nothing existed. Matter, energy, and space came into being in the Big Bang. So did time.

Astronomers are not so sure about how the universe will end. They think it will probably carry on expanding forever, gradually running out of energy. Alternatively, one day it might stop expanding and start to shrink. It will get smaller and smaller until it crushes itself out of existence in an event astronomers call the Big Crunch. But even this might not be the end. Perhaps another Big Bang will create another universe. We shall never know.

STAR RAYS

In the searing hot interior of stars, nuclear reactions take place that provide the energy to make them shine. Stars give out energy not only as light but also in the form of many other kinds of rays, such as infrared (heat) rays and radio waves.

Top right: Radio telescopes are fitted with huge metal dishes to gather the faint radio signals that reach Earth from heavenly bodies.

Center right: Satellites are sent into space to pick up infrared rays from the stars. This is IRAS, which operated in 1983.

Right: Domed buildings like this are a familiar sight at astronomical observatories. They house powerful telescopes, which gather the feeble light from the stars with large mirrors. At night the dome rolls back, and the astronomers train the telescope on the starry heavens. Usually they take photographs of the stars, using the telescopes like cameras.

We gain most of our information about the stars by studying the faint light they give out. We can tell such things as how hot they are, what chemical elements they contain, and how fast they are moving.

However, studying light tells us only part of the story about what a star or a galaxy is really like. Light is just one form of energy that stars give out. And light is the form our eyes are sensitive to.

Stars also give out energy in the form of other kinds of radiation, such as gamma rays, X-rays, infrared rays, ultraviolet rays, microwaves, and radio waves.

THE ELECTROMAGNETIC FAMILY

All these other rays belong to the same family of rays as light. They are electromagnetic waves – electric and magnetic vibrations in space. The main difference between them lies in the length of their waves, or as scientists say, their wavelengths. Gamma rays have a very short wavelength – several billion waves could fit into a yard. Radio waves have the longest wavelength – up to several miles.

Of these other star rays, we can only study radio waves on Earth, because they are the only ones that can pass through the atmosphere. The other rays are blocked by it. Since the Space Age began, however, astronomers have been able to send their telescopes and instruments into space on satellites. Hundreds of miles above the Earth, these astronomical satellites are clear of the atmosphere and can view the heavens at all wavelengths. They give Earth-bound astronomers quite a different view of the universe from usual.

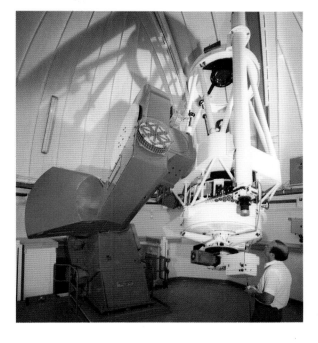

Right: This is a modern reflecting (mirror) telescope called the Jacobus Kapteyn (after a Dutch astronomer 1851–1922). Like all modern instruments it works under computer control. Its mirror is 1 metre (3.3-feet) in diameter. This telescope is sited at one of the world's newest observatories, the Roque de los Muchachos, on the island of La Palma, in the Canary Isles.

THE STARS

TELESCOPES

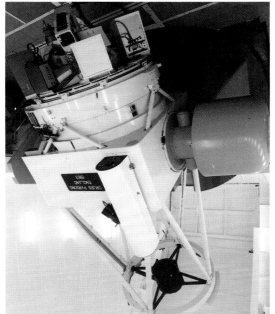

We cannot learn much about the stars just by looking at them with our eyes. Our eyes are too small and not sensitive enough. To improve our vision, we must use a telescope, or binoculars, which are a kind of double-barreled telescope. Telescopes gather much more light than our eyes and make visible faint stars we cannot normally see.

Some astronomical telescopes use lenses to gather and focus starlight. They are called refractors. The biggest ones, however, use curved mirrors instead. They are called

Above: A view of the Roque de los Muchachos Observatory at La Palma, in the Canary Islands. It is one of the finest observatory sites in Europe, which has the benefit of good weather on most nights of the year. The big dome houses Britain's Isaac Newton telescope, which has a 2.5-metre (8-foot) mirror. This instrument is shown **right.**

reflectors. The world's largest reflector is in Russia, on Mt. Semirodniki in the Caucasus Mountains. Its mirror is 20 feet across. It is so sensitive it can detect the light from a candle 15,000 miles away!

Today, professional astronomers do not usually look through their big telescopes when studying the stars. They use the telescopes instead as giant cameras to take photographs of the heavens. There is a good reason for this. Photographic film can store light. So even the faintest stars can be made to show up if the film is exposed for long enough. Sometimes the telescopes remain trained on the same part of the heavens all night. They are driven around so they follow the stars as they wheel overhead.

In order to give the clearest viewing, most astronomical observatories are located high up in the mountains. There, the telescopes are above the thickest and dustiest part of the atmosphere.

Above: One of the biggest observatories in the United States, on Kitt Peak, in the Arizona desert. The air is very dry and clear. It is hardly ever cloudy. The big dome in the picture houses the Mayall reflector, which has a mirror 4 metres (13 feet) across.

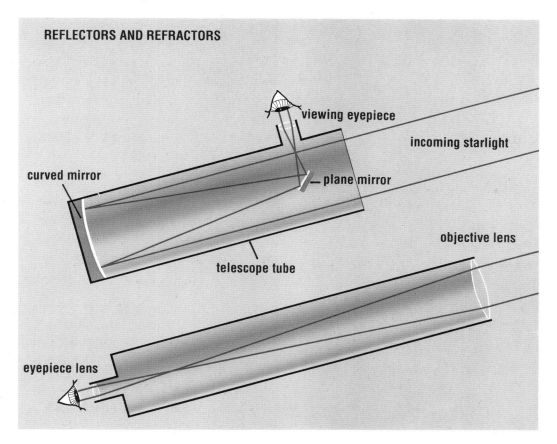

REFLECTORS AND REFRACTORS

viewing eyepiece

incoming starlight

curved mirror

plane mirror

telescope tube

objective lens

eyepiece lens

Left: The principles of simple telescopes. A reflector (top) uses a curved mirror to gather the light rays from a star. It reflects them on to a smaller plane (flat) mirror, which in turn reflects them into an eyepiece for viewing. The large objective lens of a refractor (bottom) gathers the light and forms an image, which is then viewed through the eyepiece lens.

MEASURING STARS

We know a great deal about one star because it is very close to us. It is the Sun. It is a huge ball of very hot gases, mainly hydrogen and helium. It also contains many other chemical elements, such as iron, calcium, and magnesium. Astronomers have found that most of the other stars are basically the same as the Sun.

Compared with the other stars, the Sun is not particularly bright, nor particularly large. It is classed as a yellow dwarf. There are stars tens of thousands of times brighter and others hundreds of times bigger. One of the biggest is called Betelgeuse, in the constellation Orion. It is a super giant star hundreds of millions of miles in diameter. But some white dwarf stars are only a few thousand miles across.

SPLITTING UP THE LIGHT

How do astronomers find out a star's "vital statistics"? They do this by examining starlight with various instruments. The most important one is the spectroscope. This splits up the light into a spectrum, or rainbow of color. When examined closely, the spectrum appears to be crossed by a number of dark lines. And it is these lines that hold the key to understanding the star. The dark lines show where certain wavelengths, or colors, in the starlight are absent. This happens because the outer "atmosphere" of a star absorbs these wavelengths from the light passing through.

From the number and position of the lines, astronomers can usually tell what the star is made of, how fast it is moving, and how hot, bright, or big it is. They can often use this information to figure out the distance to the star.

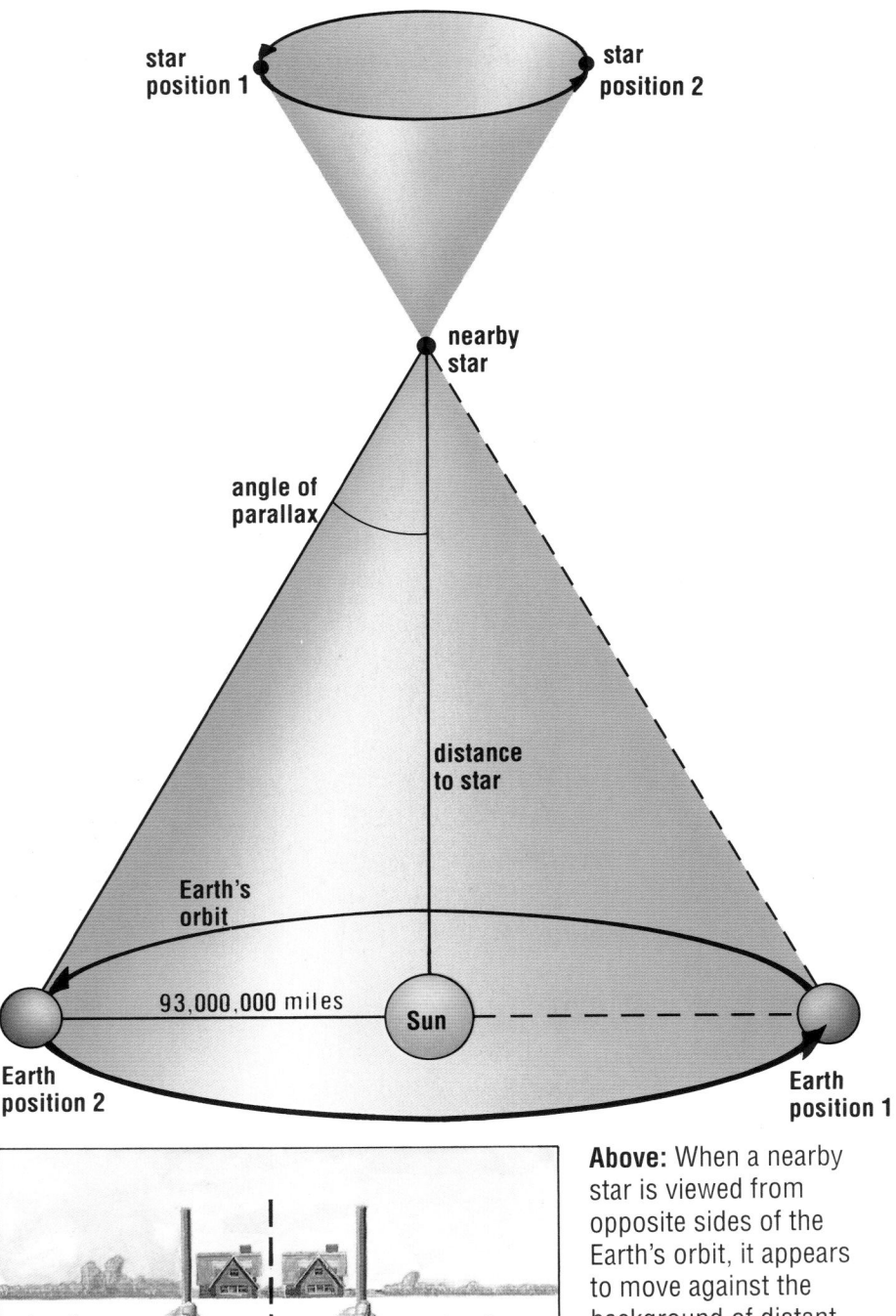

Above: When a nearby star is viewed from opposite sides of the Earth's orbit, it appears to move against the background of distant stars. This demonstrates parallax. We can work out the distance to the star by geometry.

Left: You can show the principle of parallax by holding up a pencil and looking at it first with one eye closed then the other. Notice how the pencil appears to move against the background.

Right: A cluster of stars in the southern constellation Crux – the Southern Cross. The cluster is known as the Jewel Box. Different colored stars have a different kind of spectrum. The color is a good guide to the star's surface temperature. Blue-white stars are the hottest; red stars are the coolest.

Astronomers can measure the distance to a few stars directly, using the method of parallax explained here. It works by measuring the change in position of a star against a background of distant stars. Such a change may occur when the star is viewed from opposite ends of the Earth's orbit around the Sun (see diagram). However, only a few hundred of the nearest stars show any noticeable change.

Right: The bright star in this photograph is Capella, which is in the northern constellation of Auriga. Auriga lies on the edge of the dense mass of stars we call the Milky Way. Capella is the sixth brightest star in the heavens. Its light takes 46 years to reach us.

STAR BRIGHTNESS

Each kind of star produces a different kind of spectrum. A hot, bright star produces one in which blue stands out more than red. In the spectrum of a cool, dim star, red stands out more than blue.

Astronomers group stars into a number of classes according to their spectrum. The main spectral classes are known as O, B, A, F, G, K, and M. (You will always remember them if you learn the catchy phrase: "Oh, Be A Fine Girl, Kiss Me!")

MAGNITUDES OF BRIGHTNESS

Stars vary greatly in brightness, as we can see when we look at the sky. Astronomers describe the brightness of a star by its magnitude. The brightest stars we see are called stars of the 1st magnitude; the dimmest, stars of the 6th magnitude. The other stars fall in between.

For very bright stars, the scale of magnitude is extended backwards to minus values. For example, Sirius, the brightest star in the heavens, has a magnitude of −1.45. For stars too faint for our eyes to see, the scale is extended forward. For example, the very faint Proxima Centauri, the star closest to us, has a magnitude of 11.

These magnitudes refer to the brightness of the stars as we see them. But the stars are all at different distances. This means that what we see as a dim star may not really be dim at all. It may be a bright star that lies far away.

The only way astronomers can really compare the brightness of stars is to figure out what their brightness would be at a standard distance. This is how astronomers get their scale of true brightness, or absolute magnitude.

The absolute magnitude and the

THE 10 BRIGHTEST STARS

Name	Constellation	Visible Magnitude
Sirius	Canis Major	−1.45
Canopus	Carina	−0.7
Alpha Centauri	Centaurus	−0.2
Arcturus	Boötes	−0.1
Vega	Lyra	0.0
Capella	Auriga	0.1
Rigel	Orion	0.1
Procyon	Canis Minor	0.4
Achernar	Eridanus	0.5
Beta Centauri	Centaurus	0.6

THE 10 NEAREST STARS

Name	Constellation	Distance (light-years)
Proxima Centauri	Centaurus	4.28
Alpha Centauri	Centaurus	4.3
Barnard's star	Ophiuchus	5.9
Wolf 359	Leo	7.6
Lalande 21185	Ursa Major	8.1
Sirius	Canis Major	8.8
UV Ceti	Cetus	8.9
Ross 154	Sagittarius	9.5
Ross 248	Andromeda	10.3
Eta Eridani	Eridanus	10.8

spectral class are two of the most distinct features of a star. When they are plotted against each other on a graph, interesting things happen, as you can see here.

THE H-R DIAGRAM

The first astronomers to discover the relationship between the absolute magnitude and spectral class of stars were Eijnar Hertzsprung in Denmark, and Henry N. Russell in the USA. And the graph relating the two is called the Hertzsprung-Russell diagram in their honor.

One version of the diagram is shown opposite. It shows spectral class plotted against luminosity, which is the true brightness of a star compared with that of the Sun. By far the majority of the stars lie in a broad diagonal band, which is called the main sequence. The Sun and the brightest star in the sky, Sirius, both lie in it.

Right: The Hertzsprung-Russell diagram on which some of the brightest and nearest stars are plotted. The brightest stars are more than 10,000 (10^4) times brighter than the Sun. The brightness of the most dim stars is less than 1/10,000th (10^{-4}) that of the Sun. Most stars lie in the main sequence. They are in the prime of life. The stars off the main sequence are dying.

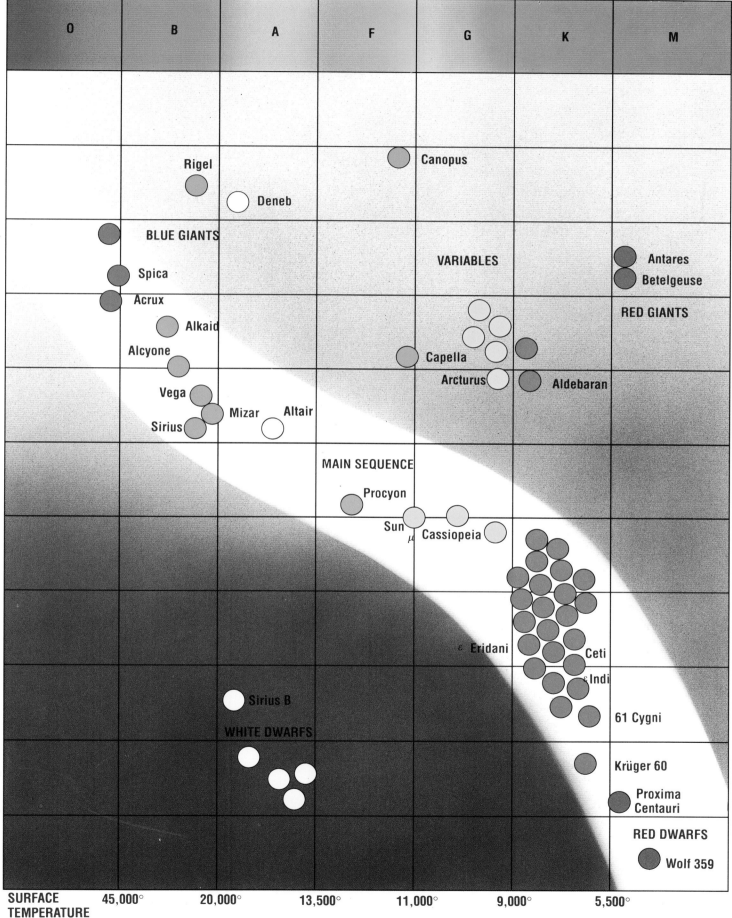

SPECTRAL TYPE

| O | B | A | F | G | K | M |

Rigel

Canopus

Deneb

BLUE GIANTS

VARIABLES

Antares

Spica

Betelgeuse

Acrux

RED GIANTS

Alkaid

Alcyone

Capella

Vega

Arcturus

Aldebaran

Mizar   Altair

Sirius

MAIN SEQUENCE

Procyon

Sun
μ   Cassiopeia

ε Eridani

Ceti

ε Indi

Sirius B

61 Cygni

WHITE DWARFS

Krüger 60

Proxima
Centauri

RED DWARFS

Wolf 359

LUMINOSITY (SUN=1)

SURFACE
TEMPERATURE

45,000°   20,000°   13,500°   11,000°   9,000°   5,500°

21

COMPANIONS

The stars that make the patterns we call the constellations are not in fact grouped together in space. They just happen to lie in the same part of the sky as we view them from Earth. But stars do group together in space in small and large numbers.

The Sun travels through space alone. But two out of every three stars travel with one or more companions. Many are double stars, which astronomers call binary stars or binaries. They consist of two stars circling around each other. One of the best-known binaries is Mizar, the middle star in the "handle" of the constellation we call the Big Dipper. A telescope shows that it is actually two stars, circling close together.

Sometimes we see the stars in a binary system eclipse, or pass in front of one another. When this happens, the overall brightness of the system suddenly drops. The star appears to wink at us. The first of these eclipsing binaries to be discovered was the star Algol, in the constellation Perseus. It is nicknamed the "Winking demon."

CLUSTERING TOGETHER
Sometimes stars group together on a much larger scale to form what is called a cluster. If you look in the northern constellation Taurus, you can easily spot one cluster with the naked eye. It is called the Pleiades, or Seven Sisters. It is an example of an open cluster and contains up to 200 stars. But we can see only six or seven with the naked eye. In binoculars the Pleiades is a glorious sight. Like most open clusters it is made up of young

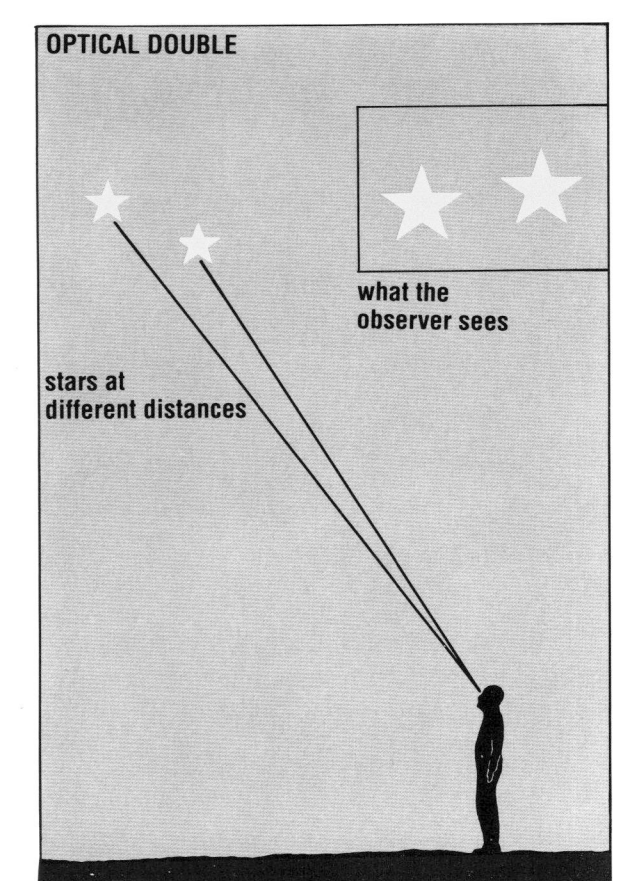

OPTICAL DOUBLE

stars at different distances

what the observer sees

Left: In many parts of the sky we can see stars that have a close companion. We call them double stars. But most of them do not lie close together in space. They appear close together only because they lie in the same direction. We call these pairs of stars optical doubles.

Below: In a double-star system called an eclipsing binary, the two stars regularly pass in front of each other as we view them from Earth. This causes the brightness of the system to vary. When one is bigger and dimmer than the other, the change can be considerable.

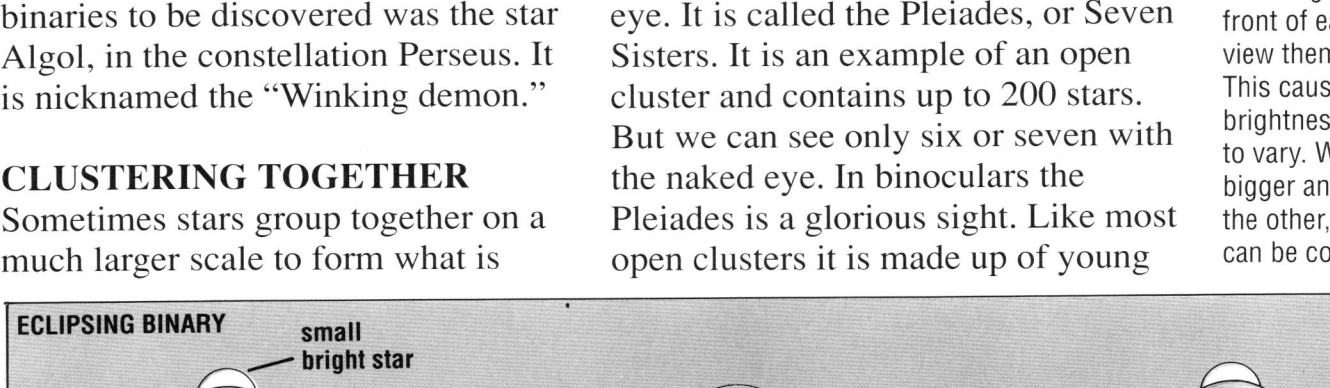

ECLIPSING BINARY

small bright star

large dim star

primary eclipse

secondary eclipse

primary eclipse

brightness curve

days   0   1   2   3

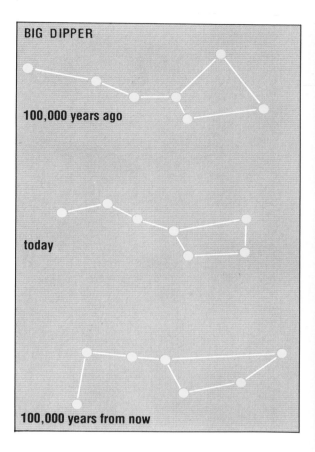

BIG DIPPER

100,000 years ago

today

100,000 years from now

Above: The Big Dipper is one of the most familiar of all constellations. But its shape is gradually changing because its stars are not grouped together in space and are moving in different directions.

Above right: An open cluster of stars in the Southern Hemisphere. They are mostly very hot blue-giant stars.

Right: This globular cluster is known as M3. It is a globe-shaped mass of old stars in the northern constellation Canes Venatici.

stars, which formed in the past few million years.

Stargazers in the Southern Hemisphere can easily see another kind of cluster with the naked eye. It is called Omega Centauri, in the constellation Centaurus. It is made up of thousands of stars gathered in a globe shape. It is an example of a globular cluster. About 125 globular clusters are known, mostly lying in the direction of the center of our Galaxy in far southern skies. They are made up of very old stars.

NEBULAE

Most of the matter in the universe is contained in the stars. The space between the stars is almost empty - almost, but not quite. There are, here and there, traces of dust and gas. We call them interstellar matter: the word interstellar means "between the stars." Sometimes the matter is thick enough to be visible. And we see it as a cloud, or nebula.

When there is a star nearby, it may cause the nebula to light up. We can see these bright nebulae in many of the constellations. Through a telescope, they look like gigantic flames, as if the heavens were on fire. Many of the nebulae are flaming red, because that is the color of the radiation given off by the hydrogen gas they contain.

Some nebulae have a distinctive ring shape, such as the Ring nebula in the constellation Lyra. It is not an ordinary nebula, but a ring of gas puffed out by a central star. We call this type a planetary nebula.

Many nebulae are not lit up by stars, and do not normally show up. But we can see them if they happen to lie between us and a starry part of the sky. Then they blot out the light of the stars behind them, and we see them as black "holes" in the heavens. We call them dark nebulae. There is one near the bright stars that form the constellation of the Southern Cross.

Right: A great dust cloud found near one of the stars in the "belt" of the constellation Orion. Part of the cloud glows brightly because of the energy absorbed from nearby stars. The dark region shows where thick dust is blocking the light from distant stars. Note the distinctive shape of the dark cloud where it breaks into the bright region. It is called the Horsehead Nebula.

Below: Looking towards the center of our Galaxy, in the constellation Sagittarius, the stars appear to be closely packed together. They form what are called star clouds. This region also looks cloudy because it contains large amounts of dust.

STAR BIRTH

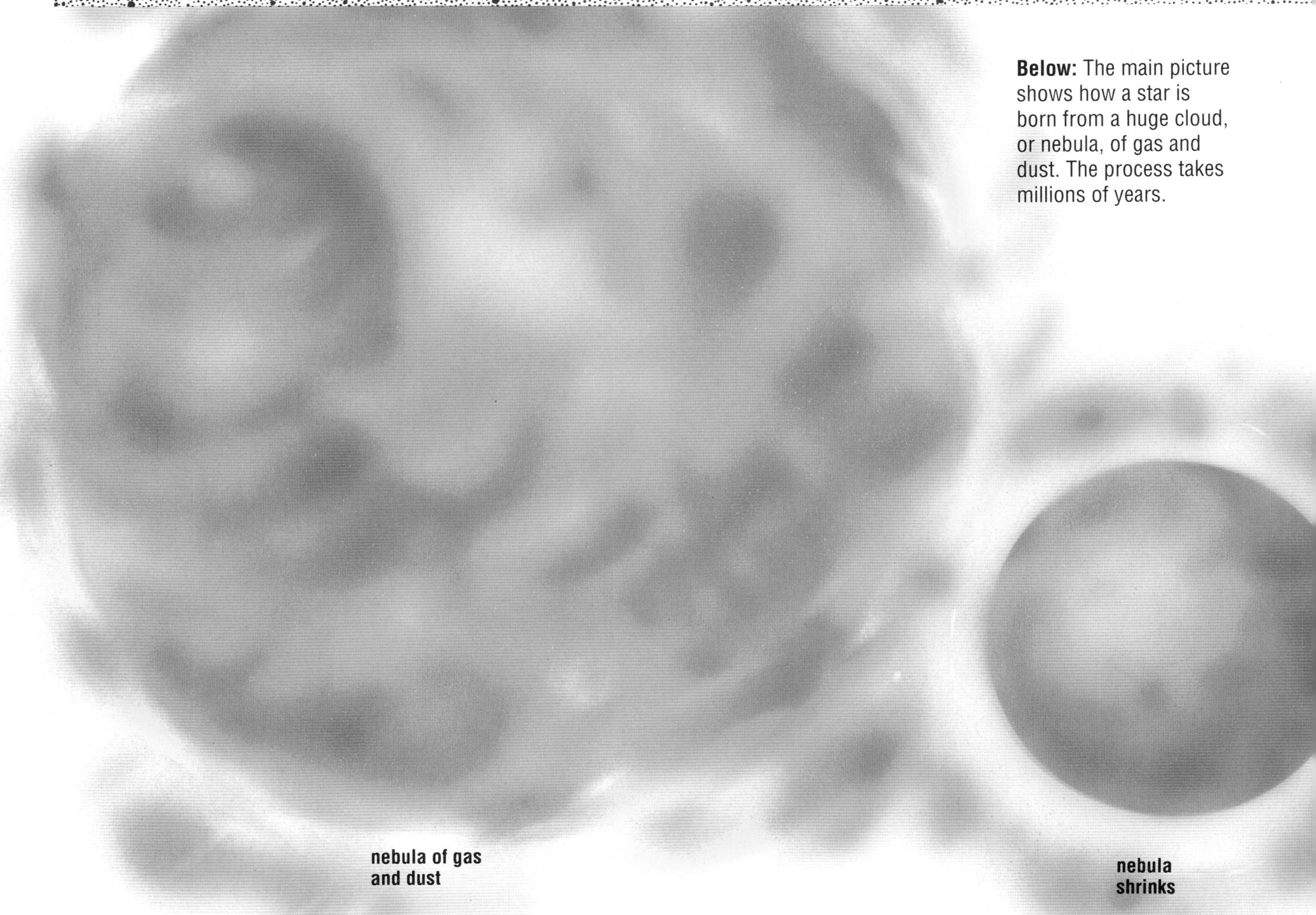

Below: The main picture shows how a star is born from a huge cloud, or nebula, of gas and dust. The process takes millions of years.

nebula of gas
and dust

nebula
shrinks

We might think that the stars are everlasting because the heavens never seem to change. But they are not. All the time new stars are being born and old ones are dying. Stars live out their lives just as we do. But whereas our lives are numbered in tens of years, the lives of stars are numbered in thousands of millions of years.

Stars are born in the great clouds of gas and dust we call nebulae. In parts of these clouds, gas and dust suddenly start coming together. Gravity, the pull of one piece of matter to another, causes this to happen. As the process continues, the cloud shrinks and eventually forms into a ball shape. The more it shrinks, the hotter it gets.

Below: Enormous amounts of energy are produced inside stars when the nuclei (centers) of hydrogen atoms combine. This creates a new element – helium.

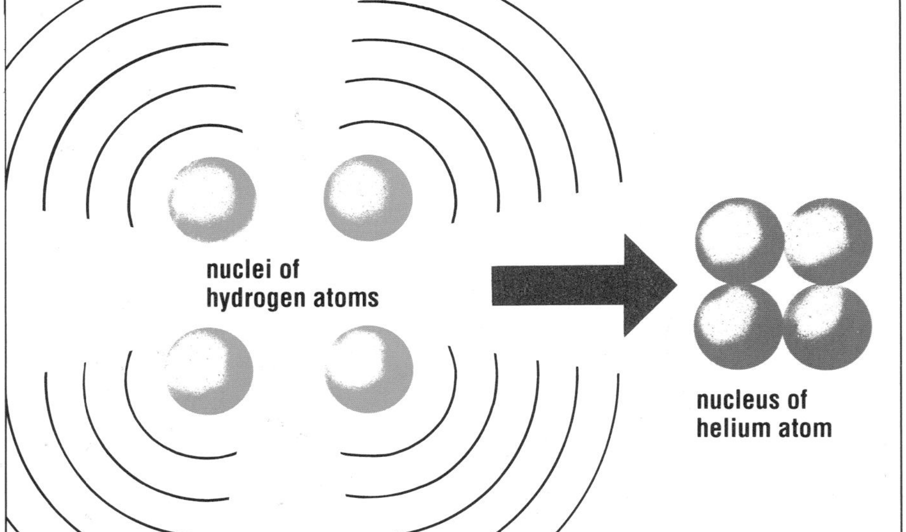

nuclei of
hydrogen atoms

nucleus of
helium atom

THE NUCLEAR FURNACE

Even the temperature inside the shrinking ball of matter increases to many millions of degrees. This is hot enough to cause atoms of the hydrogen gas present to combine, or fuse together. They combine to form another element, helium.

This process, called nuclear fusion, produces enormous amounts of energy as light and heat. The ball of matter starts to shine, and a new star is born. Soon it stops shrinking, and shines with a steady light. It will continue doing this for many millions of years until its hydrogen "fuel" runs out.

Our own star, the Sun, has been shining steadily for about 5,000 million years. During this time it has been using up to 4 million tons of hydrogen every second! But it is so big there is enough fuel left to last for thousands of millions of years to come. Stars with a smaller mass than the Sun have an even longer life, while stars with a much bigger mass have a much shorter life.

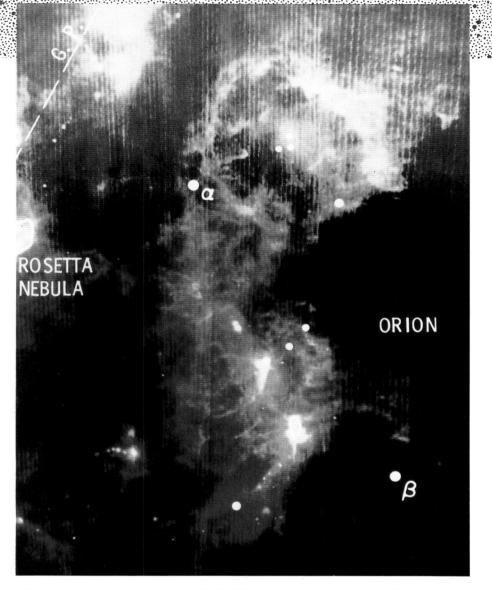

Above: The astronomical satellite IRAS took this photograph of the Great Nebula in Orion. As it was able to detect infrared radiation, IRAS provided a new view of the center of the Milky Way.

nuclear reactions begin

a star is born

STAR DEATH

a star like the Sun

star expands

Right: Astronomers think that the biggest stars form black holes when they die. Around a black hole gravity is so great that nothing can escape from it, not even light.

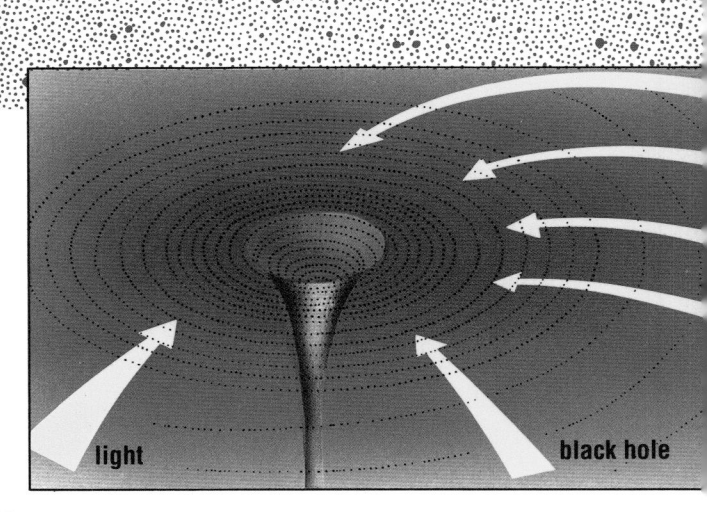

light

black hole

red giant

star shrinks

When a star runs out of its hydrogen fuel, it begins to collapse under gravity. This causes it to heat up. When it gets hot enough, new kinds of nuclear fusion processes begin. The energy given out makes the star expand a hundred times or more. It becomes what is called a red giant.

What happens next depends on how massive the star is. A star like the Sun stays at the red giant stage for some time and then gradually shrinks. It gets smaller and smaller and whiter and whiter, until it is not much bigger

than the Earth. It is now a white dwarf. It is incredibly dense: a lump the size of a sugar cube would weigh a ton or more!

A star more massive than the Sun grows much bigger than a red giant and becomes a super giant. In time the super giant collapses. This releases so much energy that a massive explosion takes place, blasting the star apart. We call this explosion a supernova.

After a supernova, what is left of the star collapses into a tiny ball made up of atomic particles called neutrons.

white dwarf

Above: A relatively small star like the Sun shines steadily for about 10,000 million years. Then it swells up into a red giant. This will gradually shrink until it becomes a tiny white dwarf, which in time will fade and become invisible.

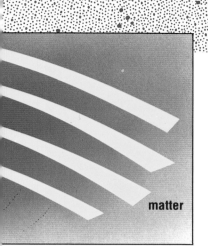

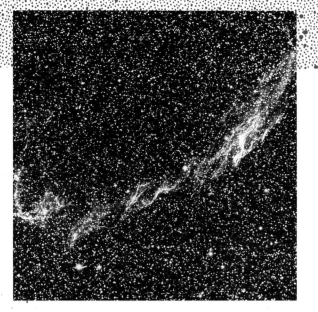

It is even smaller and denser than a white dwarf. It may give out beams of radio waves as it rotates. We detect them as radio pulses. This body is called a pulsar.

Very massive stars continue to collapse until there is no matter left. A region of enormous gravity remains with a pull so great that it attracts and "swallows" anything nearby, even light. We call it a black hole.

matter

Below: Massive stars expand into supergiant stars, before they explode as a supernova.

Above: These wisps of glowing dust in the constellation Cygnus form the Veil nebula. It is what remains of a supernova explosion that happened 30,000 years ago.

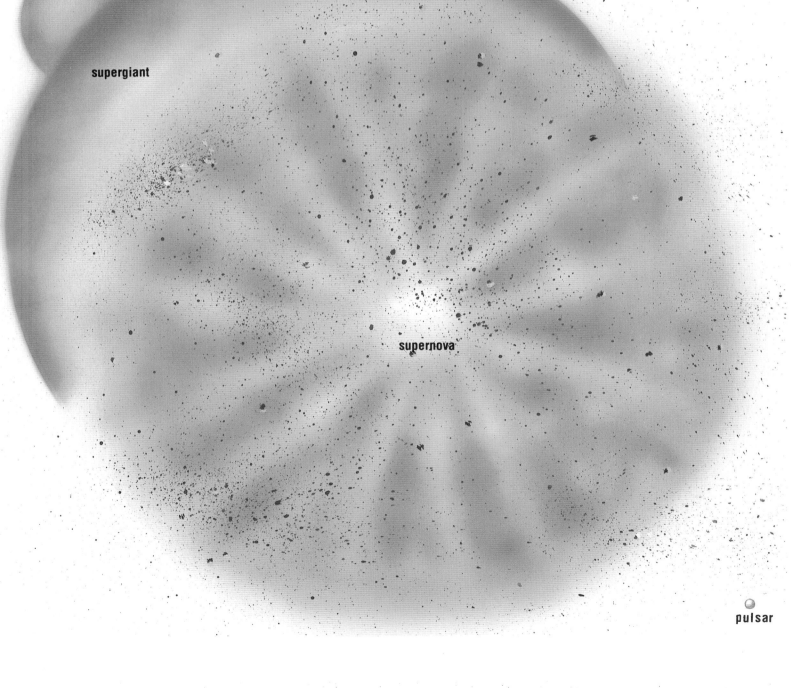

massive star

supergiant

supernova

pulsar

DEATH OF THE SUN

The Sun was born from a cloud of gas and dust about 5,000 million years ago. At the same time its family of planets came into being, including the Earth. About 3,000 million years ago, the first traces of life appeared on Earth. But human beings did not appear until about 3 million years ago.

Humankind and all life depend entirely on the Sun for their existence. It provides living things with the light and warmth they need to survive.

So what will happen to the Earth and the life upon it when the Sun begins to die, as one day it must? We have a long time to think about this because it will not happen for another 5,000 million years!

When the Sun does begin to die, it will gradually start to expand, growing redder and brighter as it does so. The temperature on Earth will start to rise. The polar ice caps will melt, causing worldwide flooding. The crops will fail as farmland is baked into desert. Much later the oceans will turn into steam. Later still the air in the atmosphere will be driven off into space.

By then the Sun will have reached its full red-giant size. It will have swallowed the planet Mercury and maybe even Venus.

All life on Earth will have perished by that time. But by then Earth people will have left. They will have solved the problem of interstellar flight and will be living on Earth-like planets in other solar systems in other parts of our Galaxy.

In 5,000 million years' time this is what could become of the Earth. The huge red-giant Sun, now very much closer, will be roasting our planet. The ground will split and shake as violent earthquakes occur and volcanoes erupt. Traces of the human race will disappear.

GALAXIES

Above: From far out in space, this is what our Galaxy would look like. Most of the stars are clustered together on long, curved arms, which come out of the central bulge. The Galaxy is about 100,000 light-years across. The Sun lies on one of the arms, about 30,000 light-years from the center.

The Sun and all the stars we see in the night sky belong to a great family of stars that journeys through space together. We call such a family, a galaxy. There are many billions of galaxies in the universe. We call our star family, the Milky Way Galaxy, or often just the Galaxy. The word "galaxy" comes from the Greek word meaning milk.

We know that our Sun is far away from the center of the Galaxy, which lies in the constellation Sagittarius.

When you gaze at the heavens on a really dark night, you can see a misty band of light arching across the sky. We call this the Milky Way, too. There is a very good reason for this. If you look at this band in a telescope, you can see that it is made up of masses of stars apparently squashed close together. What you are, in fact, looking at is a slice through the densest part of the Milky Way Galaxy.

Above: The great galaxy in the constellation Andromeda. It is one of the few galaxies we can see with the naked eye. It is much bigger than our own, but its shape is very similar. It lies over 2 million light-years away.

Inset: This is what our Galaxy would look like viewed from the side. The center bulge measures about 20,000 light-years across.

TWO FRIED EGGS

The Galaxy is a huge disc with a bulge in the middle. It has often been described as being shaped like two fried eggs placed back to back! The stars are not spread evenly across the disc. They gather on long "arms" that curve out from the center bulge. The whole disc is spinning around as it rushes headlong through space. From a distance it would look like a flaming Catherine Wheel firework.

The Galaxy is enormous. It is the home of some 100,000 million stars. A beam of light takes 100,000 years to travel from one edge of the disc to the other.

But the Galaxy is not very special as far as the universe is concerned, although it is one of the largest of its type. There are many others like it. Some are even bigger. But they all contain the same kinds of stars, clusters, and clouds of gas and dust.

GALAXY FAMILIES

E0

ELLIPTICAL GALAXIES

E3

E7

A method of classifying the galaxies according to their shape, first suggested by the astronomer Edwin Hubble. Some of the biggest galaxies are ellipticals (E), they may be round or oval. Spirals (S) are classed a, b or c according to how open the arms are. Barred spirals (SB), which have a bar through the center, are also classed a, b and c. Our own Galaxy is an Sb type.

Our Galaxy, the Milky Way, has its stars arranged on arms that curve out from the center bulge. It is a type we call a spiral galaxy. One of our neighbors in space, the Andromeda Galaxy, is another spiral. In fact, spirals are very common in the universe. But they are not all alike. In some spiral galaxies the arms are much closer together than in our own Galaxy. In others, the arms are more wide open.

Another type of spiral galaxy is very different. It has the spiral arms coming from a band of stars that passes through the center. We call this type a barred-spiral galaxy.

Some galaxies have no arms at all. They are either round or oval in shape, and are known as ellipticals.

PIONEER OF THE GALAXIES

Until early this century, no one knew that there were such things as other galaxies. Astronomers thought that our Galaxy made up the entire universe. They had found certain misty patches in some parts of the heavens, but thought these were just peculiar nebulae in our Galaxy.

Then, in the 1920s, astronomers began working with the powerful new 100 inch reflecting telescope at Mt. Wilson Observatory in California.

They proved beyond any doubt that the peculiar misty patches were separate galaxies very far away. They were often called extragalactic nebulae.

The astronomer who did most of the pioneering work at Mt. Wilson was Edwin Hubble. It was Hubble who first classed galaxies into ellipticals, spirals, and barred spirals. He thought ellipticals formed first and later developed into spirals. We now know, however, this does not happen. No one is certain exactly how galaxies form and develop.

Sa

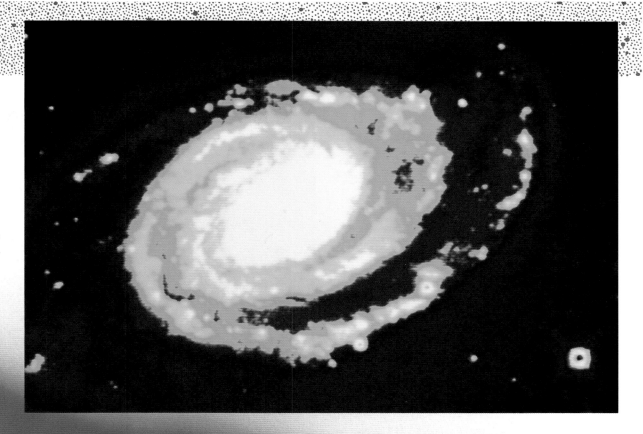

Right: This is a spiral galaxy of the Sc type, with arms quite wide apart. It is found in the constellation Virgo. False colors have been used in the picture to show different levels of brightness.

BARRED-SPIRAL GALAXIES

SBb

SBc

RAL GALAXIES

Sb

Sc

IRREGULAR GALAXIES

Most galaxies are too far away for us to see with the naked eye. But we can see one or two. In the Northern Hemisphere, we can see one as a faint misty patch in the constellation Andromeda. In the Southern Hemisphere, we can see two larger and brighter misty patches, which also turn out to be galaxies.

We call them the Large and Small Magellanic Clouds. They are named after the famous explorer Magellan, who was one of the first Europeans to see them. Unlike the Andromeda Galaxy, the Magellanic Clouds have no particular shape. We call them irregulars.

They are by far the nearest of the outer galaxies. The Large Magellanic Cloud is only about 170,000 light-years away. This compares with over 2,000,000 light-years for Andromeda. Even so, Andromeda is still a neighbor considering the vast size of the universe.

Our own Galaxy, the Magellanic Clouds, and the Andromeda Galaxy all belong to a group of galaxies, known as the Local Group. Other galaxies are grouped together in a similar way. In some parts of the heavens there are great clusters containing thousands of galaxies. Some of these galaxies appear to be colliding with one another or are joined in some way. The Toadstool galaxies are an example. The galaxy Centaurus A was once thought to be two galaxies colliding, but it turns out to be a peculiar galaxy cut in half by a thick band of dust.

Right: One of the most easily recognizable of all galaxies, Centaurus A. It appears to be cut through the middle. The "cut" is in fact a band of thick dust, which blocks the light coming from the stars behind it.

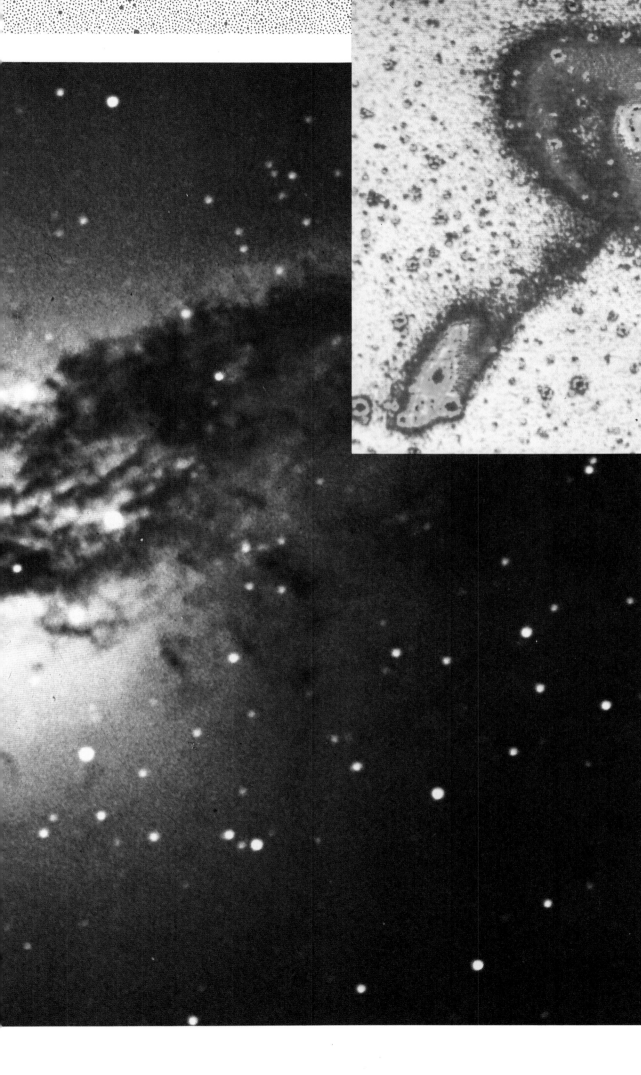

Above: These two galaxies are called the Toadstool galaxies because of their shape. They are unusual because they are connected by a bridge of hydrogen gas. False colors have been used to bring out this hydrogen link. Such galaxies are called interacting galaxies.

RADIO GALAXIES

Above: The radio telescope at Parkes in New South Wales, Australia. It uses a dish 210 feet across to collect radio waves from space. The Parkes radio observatory is particularly noted for its study of the mysterious bodies known as quasars.

T he galaxy Centaurus A, pictured on the previous page, is an example of an elliptical galaxy. But it is not like most of the others. This is because it gives out powerful beams of radio waves. It is called a radio galaxy. Many radio galaxies are known, but few are more powerful than Centaurus A.

Radio galaxies are one of the new kinds of objects astronomers discovered when they began looking at the heavens with radio telescopes. Radio astronomy began in the 1930s

when scientists found that certain interference on radio sets was coming from the heavens. Now it is one of the most exciting branches of astronomy.

Most radio telescopes are big metal dishes, which gather radio waves from the heavens in much the same way as a reflecting telescope gathers light rays. Two of the biggest are at Arecibo in Puerto Rico and Effelsberg in Germany.

The radio picture of a galaxy is quite different from one taken with light. The radio waves usually come

Below: The radio telescope near Arecibo on the Caribbean island of Puerto Rico. It has a dish 1,000 feet in diameter, set into a natural bowl in the hills. The dish is constructed of nearly 39,000 panels of aluminium mesh. **Right:** From underneath, you can see through the mesh to the receiving antenna.

from regions of space on either side of the part of the galaxy we can see.

Radio astronomers have also found curious objects known as quasars – short for quasi-stellar radio source. Quasars are much brighter than galaxies, yet much smaller. They appear to be almost like a star, which is what quasi-stellar means.

Quasars are much farther away than ordinary galaxies. Some appear to be more than 13,000 million light-years away. This is near the edge of the known universe.

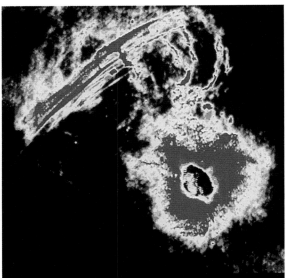

Left: Using computers, the radio signals given out by heavenly bodies can be turned into images. This is an image produced from signals from a strong radio source called Sagittarius A, near the center of our Galaxy.

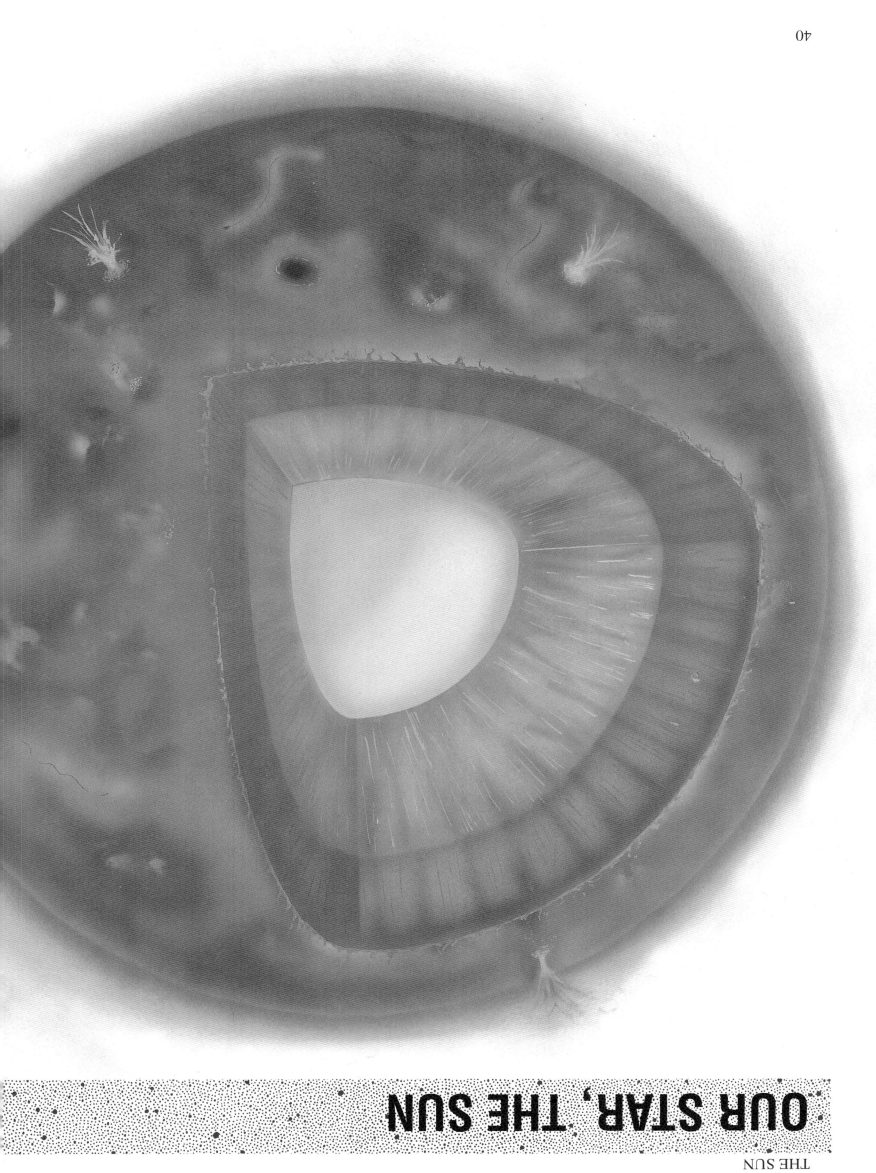

OUR STAR, THE SUN

Above: The Sun often sends out fountains of flaming gas called prominences.

Left: The exterior and interior of the Sun. The energy that keeps the Sun shining is produced in the central core. It travels slowly to the surface, and is then radiated into space as heat, light, and other radiation.

Below: In 1973, the Skylab astronauts photographed many spectacular prominences, including the one shown here. It is a false-color image, with the colors showing different levels of brightness.

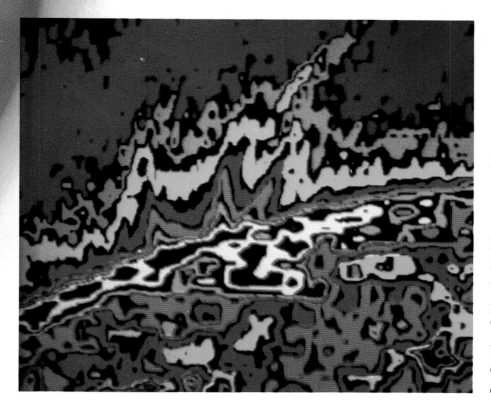

The star we know as the Sun is the source of life on the Earth. Without its light and warmth, our planet would be dark, cold, and lifeless. The Sun lies nearly 93 million miles from Earth.

Every morning the Sun rises in the east, then arches across the sky, and in the evening sets in the west. But the Sun only appears to move. In reality, it is the Earth that moves, spinning in space on its axis every 24 hours.

The Earth also has another motion in relation to the Sun. It orbits, or circles, around the Sun once every 365¼ days, the period we call a year. It orbits in this way because it is a planet, held in its place by the Sun's powerful gravity. The Sun also holds captive eight other planets. It is the center of a family of bodies, called the solar system (see page 56).

Compared with the other bodies, the Sun is huge. It contains 750 times more mass than all of them put together. Its diameter, about 865,000 miles, is 100 times larger than the Earth's. The surface of the Sun is a seething mass of boiling gases. The gases swell up from below, carrying with them the Sun's heat. The heat is produced by nuclear fusion reactions in the middle, or core, of the Sun, where the temperature reaches many million degrees. At the surface, however, the temperature is only about 10,000°F.

We call the visible surface of the Sun the photosphere ("light sphere"). It is often marked by darker regions called sunspots, which are signs of violent activity. Other signs are great fountains of gas, called prominences. They shoot many thousands of miles up above the surface into the Sun's outer atmosphere, which we call the corona ("crown").

THE SOLAR WIND

Above: Shimmering bands of color often appear in the sky above the Arctic and Antarctic. Known as the Northern and Southern Lights (Aurora Borealis and Aurora Australis), they are caused by particles streaming from the Sun.

he Sun pours out its enormous energy as light, heat, X-rays, radio waves, and other forms of radiation. It gives off atomic particles as well, mainly protons and electrons. These are two of the particles found in all atoms. They are both electrically charged – protons are positive, electrons are negative. Streams of these particles leave the Sun all the time, forming what we call the solar wind.

Normally the solar wind blows steadily all the time. But when sunspots occur, it blows stronger than usual. When this happens, streams of charged particles rain down on the Earth. They collide with atoms in the upper air, and cause them to give off colored light. Then we see another of nature's magnificent spectacles, the aurora. Usually we can see it only in far northern and far southern regions of the world. In the Northern

Below: This unusual photograph shows what the Northern Lights look like from space. It was taken by scientists on a Spacelab mission of the space shuttle, orbiting at about 155 miles.

Hemisphere, it is called the Northern Lights, and in the Southern Hemisphere, the Southern Lights.

The storm-force solar wind also affects the Earth in other ways. By disrupting the upper air, it upsets the layers that help reflect radio waves around the globe; long-distance radio communications suffer as a result. Such disruptions are often called magnetic storms. They may also affect compasses.

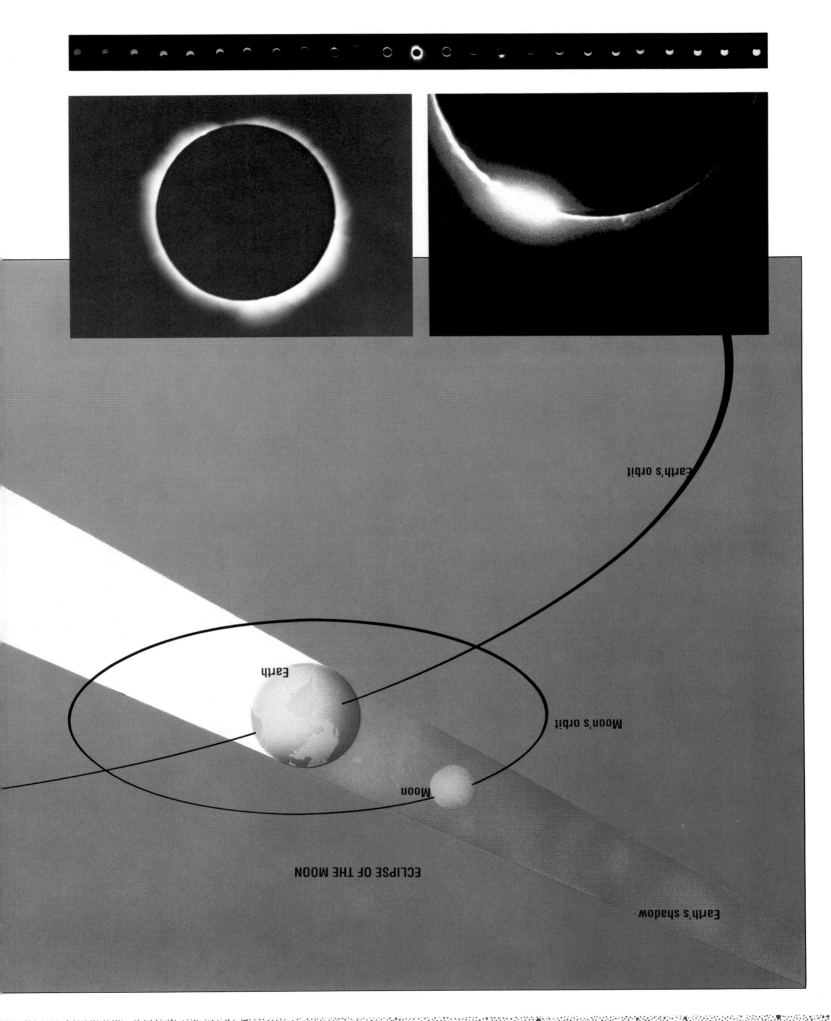

Earth's orbit

Moon's orbit

Earth

Moon

ECLIPSE OF THE MOON

Earth's shadow

ECLIPSES

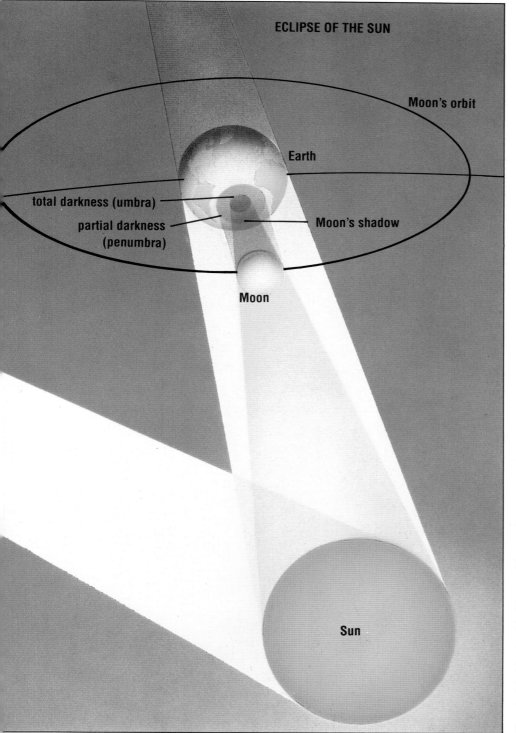

ECLIPSE OF THE SUN

Moon's orbit

Earth

total darkness (umbra)

partial darkness (penumbra)

Moon's shadow

Moon

Sun

The Earth, the Sun, and the Moon whirl around one another in space like a celestial carousel. As the Earth travels around the Sun, the Moon circles around the Earth. The Moon circles in much the same plane as the Earth. (This means that if the Sun and the Earth were on a flat sheet, the Moon would be on it, too.)

At times, therefore, the Moon moves in front of the Sun when we look from Earth. This has the result of cutting off some or all of the Sun's light. When this happens, we say an eclipse of the Sun has occurred.

Sometimes the Moon covers only part of the Sun as it moves. We call this a partial solar eclipse. When the Moon covers the whole of the Sun, we call it a total solar eclipse.

TOTALITY

During a total eclipse, the Moon blots out all of the Sun's light, making day suddenly turn into night. But only over a small area of the Earth's surface at a time, and only for a few minutes at most.

The reason for this is that the Moon is so far away that it casts only a narrow shadow on the Earth, up to about 170 miles across. As the Moon moves across the Sun, its shadow races across the Earth's surface along what is called a path of totality. On either side of the path, only a partial eclipse can be seen.

THE EARTH'S SHADOW

Just as the Moon sometimes casts its shadow on the Earth, the Earth also sometimes casts its shadow on the Moon. Then the Moon darkens, and we say a lunar eclipse has occurred. Because the Earth casts quite a broad shadow, the Moon can be in total eclipse for up to about 2½ hours.

Above: Eclipses take place when the Sun, Earth and Moon line up in space, which can happen several times a year. When the Moon comes between the Earth and the Sun, an eclipse of the Sun takes place. When the Earth comes between the Sun and the Moon, an eclipse of the Moon occurs.

Far left: Just before the Sun disappears in a total eclipse, the diamond-ring effect occurs. **Left:** During totality (total eclipse) the Sun's normally invisible corona (outer atmosphere) flashes into view.

Bottom left: This series of photographs follows the stages of an eclipse.

TOTAL ECLIPSE

Below: On 17 March 1988, the people of Bangka Island, Indonesia, welcomed astronomers who had gathered to watch a solar eclipse.

For ancient peoples a total eclipse was a terrifying event. And it is easy to see why. During totality, day becomes night; the birds stop singing and begin to roost; the air turns suddenly chilly. Even today when we know what is happening in the heavens, observing a total eclipse is an uncanny experience.

Total eclipses do not happen very often, usually less than once a year. And astronomers travel from all over the world to witness them, from the Arctic to the Tropics. They do this not only for the experience itself, but also for good scientific reasons. It is only during a total eclipse that they are able to observe certain features of the Sun, such as prominences and the corona. Usually these features are lost in the Sun's dazzling glare.

To witness the 1988 total eclipse, the author traveled nearly half-way around the world to the remote island

Below: A local boy peers through the author's camera to see the Moon start to move across the face of the Sun.

Above: At about 6 am on eclipse day, 18 March, the Sun rises behind a bank of cloud. Will the cloud spoil the eclipse?

of Bangka, off Sumatra, in Southeast Asia. The pictures on these pages record some of his experiences.

The period of totality lasted for just over two minutes but provided a never-to-be-forgotten spectacle of brilliant pink prominences and a pearly corona. All too soon these gave way to a sparkling "diamond ring," as the Sun emerged from its hiding place behind the Moon. Daylight then returned, and the birds began to sing again.

Ardent eclipse-watchers say all eclipses are different. That is why they pack up their telescopes and travel to distant parts each time heavenly geometry conspires to place the Moon in front of the Sun. In 1990, for example, they could be in Finland or Russia; in 1991, in Hawaii or Mexico; in 1992, in the South Atlantic; in 1994, in Peru or Brazil.

Below: Total eclipse. Day has turned into night. The horizon is light because daylight is already returning.

Below: Seconds before total eclipse, the Sun's light becomes feeble. The Moon's shadow races closer.

Left: The author demonstrates what is happening using lens hoods from his cameras to represent the Sun and the Moon.

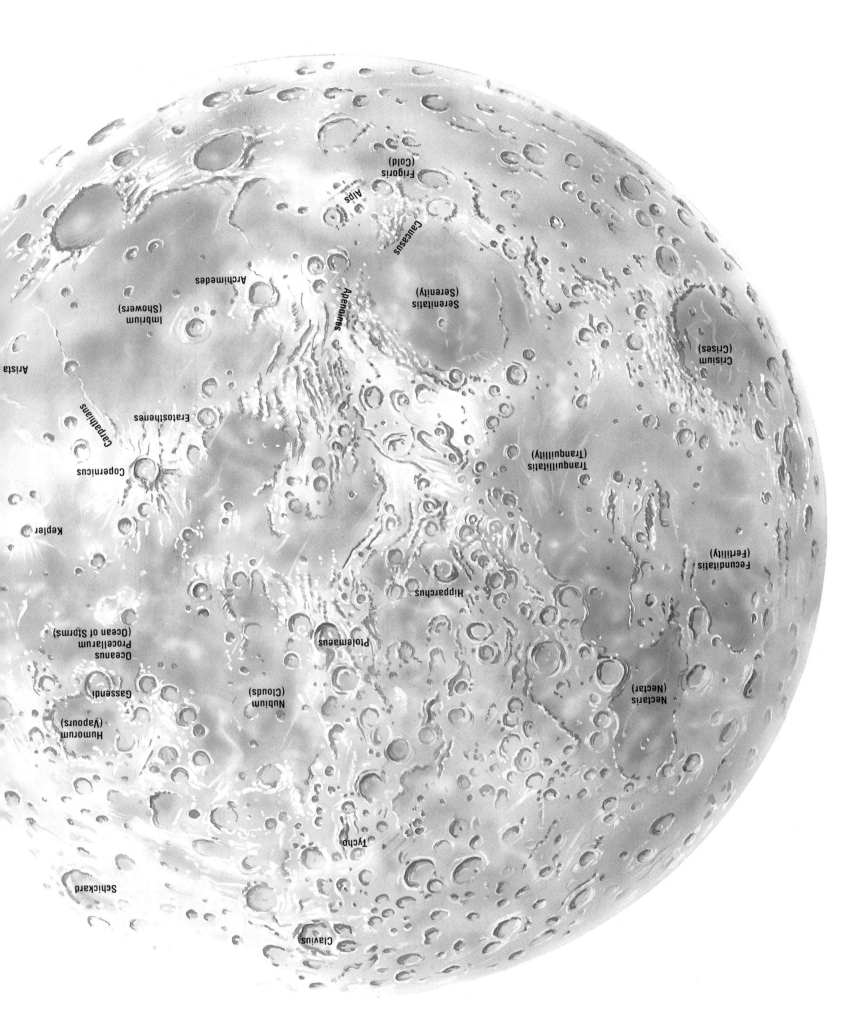

OUR NEIGHBOR, THE MOON

Left: The surface of the Moon as we see it through a telescope from Earth: south is at the top. (Through binoculars it will appear the other way up).

MARIA (SEAS)
Tranquillitatis (Tranquility)
Crisium (Crises)
Nectaris (Nectar)
Frigoris (Cold)
Nubium (Clouds)
Imbrium (Showers)
Fecunditatis (Fertility)
Humorum (Vapours)
Serenitatis (Serenity)
Oceanus Procellarum
   (Oceans of Storms)

CRATERS

Copernicus	**Tycho**
Aristarchus	**Clavius**
Hipparchus	**Schickard**
Ptolemaeus	**Grimaldi**
Archimedes	**Eratosthenes**
Kepler	**Gassendi**

MOUNTAIN RANGES

Apennines	**Caucasus**
Alps	**Carpathians**

Grimaldi

Below: A large crater on the far side of the Moon. Notice the mountains at the center. This is typical of lunar craters. The far side, which we can never see from Earth, is more heavily cratered than the near side. It has no large maria (seas).

Just as the Sun lights up the Earth during day, the Moon sometimes lightens the darkness of the night. It does so particularly when it is full, that is, when all of its surface is lit up.

At such times, even without a telescope, we can see light and dark areas on the Moon. When we have binoculars or a telescope, we can see that the light areas are rugged highlands and the dark areas are flat plains. Ancient astronomers thought that the dark areas were great oceans, and named them *maria* (singular: *mare*), meaning seas.

We still call these regions seas, even though we know they are not. There is not any water on the Moon. Nor is there any air. And where there is not any air or water, there cannot be any wind, rain or weather of any kind. Also, there cannot be any life. The Moon is a dead world.

On Earth the atmosphere, or layer of air, helps even out the temperature between day and night. But because the Moon has no atmosphere, the temperature varies greatly between day and night. In the full Sun the temperature can soar to more than 212°F the temperature of boiling water. But at night, the temperature can fall to more than −240°F far colder than anywhere on Earth.

The Moon is a small world. It measures only 2,160 miles across, only about a quarter the size of the Earth. It lies on average about 240,000 miles away, and is our nearest neighbor in space.

The Moon is the only other body in the solar system that human beings have explored on foot. This happened on the Apollo missions of the late 1960s and early 1970s (see page 54).

PHASES OF THE MOON

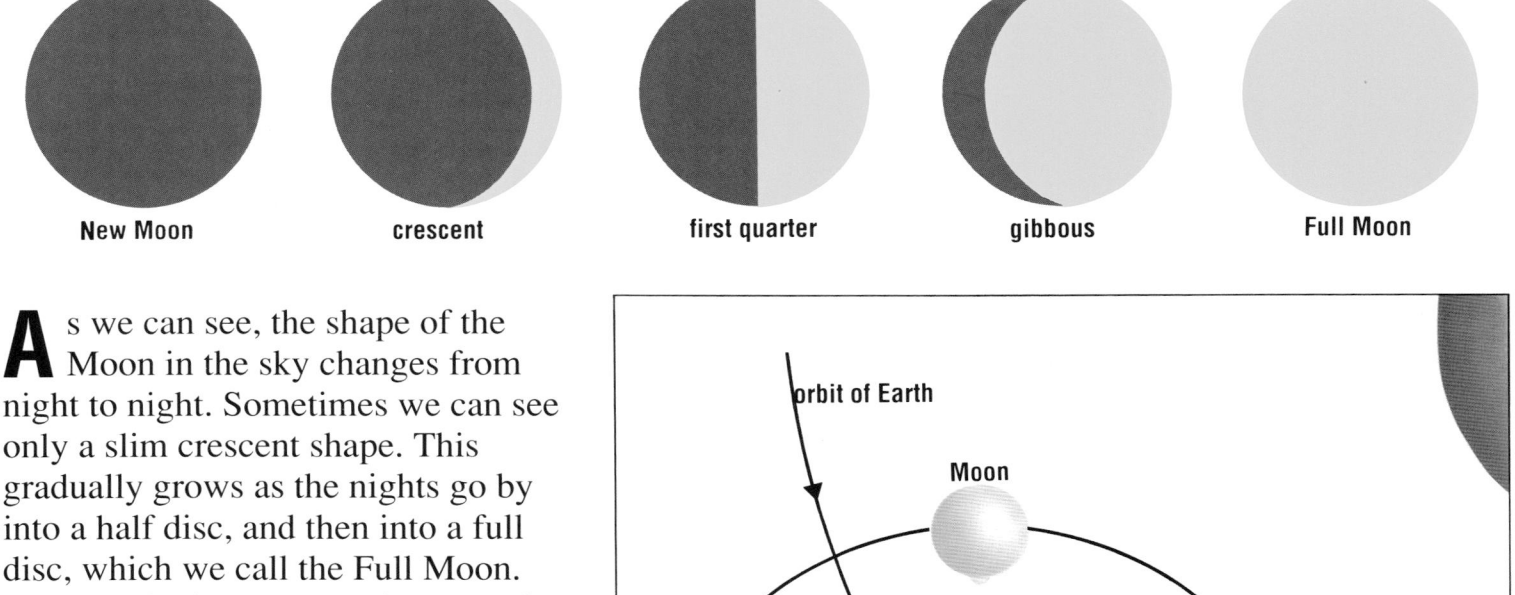

New Moon   crescent   first quarter   gibbous   Full Moon

As we can see, the shape of the Moon in the sky changes from night to night. Sometimes we can see only a slim crescent shape. This gradually grows as the nights go by into a half disc, and then into a full disc, which we call the Full Moon. During this time we say the Moon is waxing.

From full, the Moon begins to shrink, through a half disc and back to a crescent. During this time we say it is waning. Finally, it disappears.

The reason the Moon appears to change shape in the night sky is that it does not give off light of its own. It shines only because it reflects light from the Sun. The shape we see depends on how the Moon is placed in relation to the Sun and the Earth.

We call the changing shapes of the Moon, its phases. The diagram helps to explain how they occur. The Moon goes through its phases, say, from one Full Moon to the next, in 29½ days. This period is one of the great natural divisions of time. It is the basis of our month.

Sometimes the Moon moves exactly into line between the Sun and the Earth and blots out the Sun's light. An eclipse of the Sun occurs (see page 45).

The Moon circles around the Earth once every 27⅓ days. It also takes exactly the same time to spin once on its axis. Because of this, the Moon always presents the same face toward us. We call this phenomenon a captive rotation.

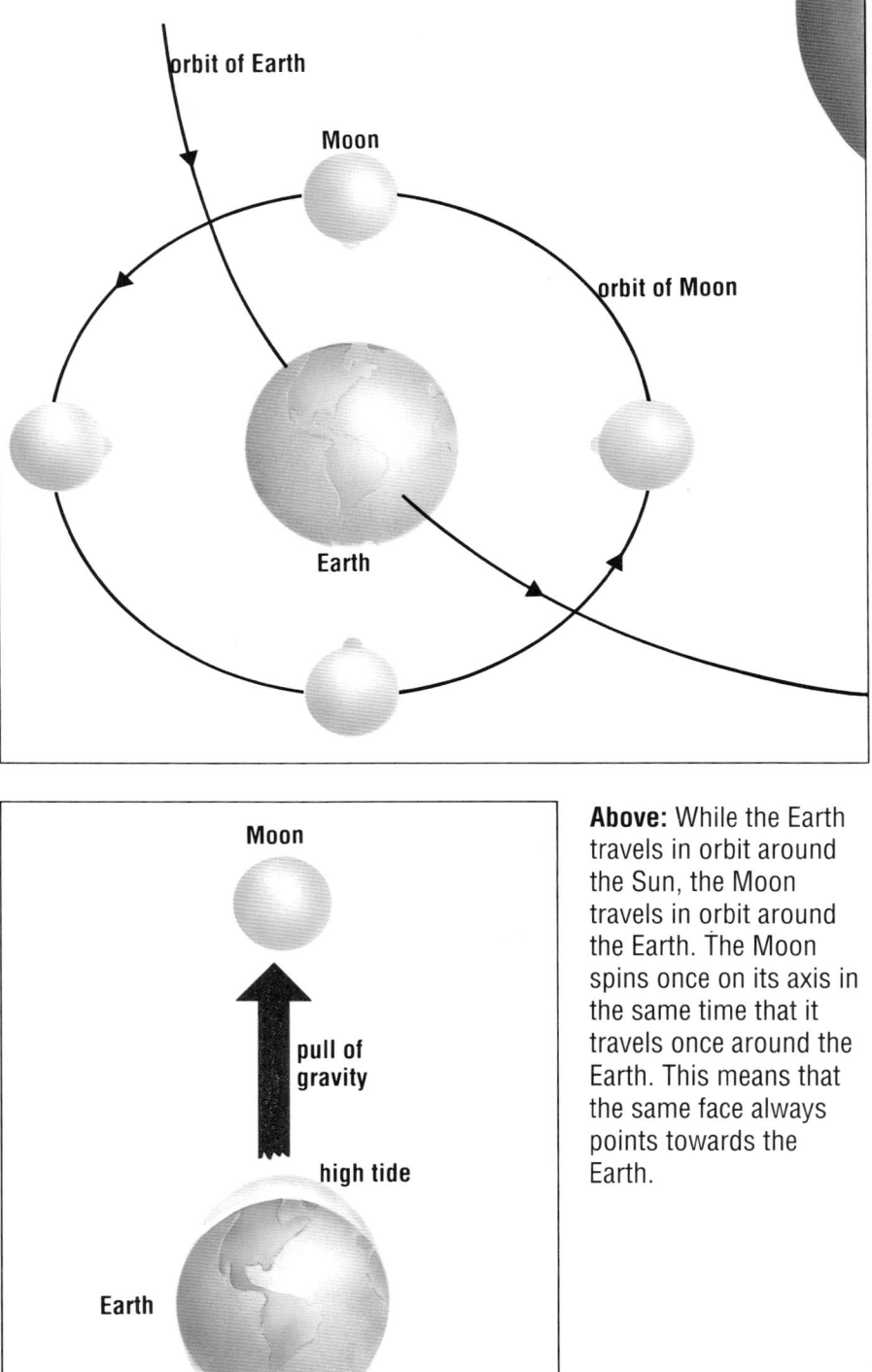

Above: While the Earth travels in orbit around the Sun, the Moon travels in orbit around the Earth. The Moon spins once on its axis in the same time that it travels once around the Earth. This means that the same face always points towards the Earth.

Left: The sea level rises when the Moon is directly overhead, creating a high tide.

50

gibbous

last quarter

crescent

New Moon

Left: The phases of the Moon. During the month the Moon appears to change shape as more or less of its surface is lit up by the Sun.

THE TIDES

The Moon has a much smaller mass than the Earth and, because of this, has a much lower force of gravity. Its "pull" is only one-sixth that of the Earth. Nevertheless, it still affects the Earth.

We see its effect most obviously at the beach, because it causes the tides to rise and fall. A high tide, for example, occurs when the Moon is overhead and "pulls" the water of the oceans toward it.

Above: The tide has gone out, and the boats appear stranded, but before long the tide will come in again. High and low tides occur twice a day.

LUNAR ODYSSEY

On July 20, 1969, one of the greatest moments in the history of humankind occurred. Two men from planet Earth set foot on another world – the Moon. They were the astronauts Neil Armstrong and Edwin Aldrin, who had traveled there in the Apollo 11 spacecraft.

Four days earlier, they had blasted off the launch pad of the Kennedy Space Center in Florida in a 365-foot tall Saturn V rocket. This had boosted their Apollo spacecraft to a speed of nearly 25,000 miles an hour – 17 times the speed of the supersonic airliner Concorde! Only at such a speed could they escape from the clutches of the Earth's gravity.

The Apollo spacecraft was made up of three parts, or modules. The three-man crew occupied the conical command module. This was attached to an equipment, or service module, forming the so-called CSM.

The third part was the lunar module. This was the part from which the two astronauts descended to the moon's surface. They took off from the Moon in the upper part of the module, using the lower one as a launch pad. Up in orbit, they rendezvoused with the CSM, which had been orbiting above them while they were exploring the surface. They then transferred to the CSM and joined their colleague for the journey back to Earth.

The three astronauts reached Earth and re-entered the atmosphere traveling as fast as they had left. Friction with the air rapidly slowed them down, making the module glow red-hot. But this is what was expected and the astronauts inside were unharmed. Eventually, parachutes opened to lower their module gently to a splashdown at sea.

People had dreamed about going to the Moon for centuries, but the technology to achieve this only became available in the 1960s. President John F. Kennedy launched the Apollo Moonlanding project in a famous speech before Congress in May 1961.

Above: The five engines of the second-stage rocket then fired, thrusting the now lighter rocket faster and faster. They burned a mixture of liquid hydrogen and liquid oxygen.

Above left: When the first stage had no fuel left, it broke away and returned to Earth. When it hit the ocean at such high speed it was smashed into pieces.

escape
tower

Apollo
spacecraft

third-stage
rocket

second-stage
rocket

first-stage
rocket

Left: The Apollo astronauts were carried into space by the biggest rocket there has ever been, the Saturn V. The five engines of the first stage of the rocket put out a thrust of over 6 million pounds. They burned a mixture of kerosene and liquid oxygen.

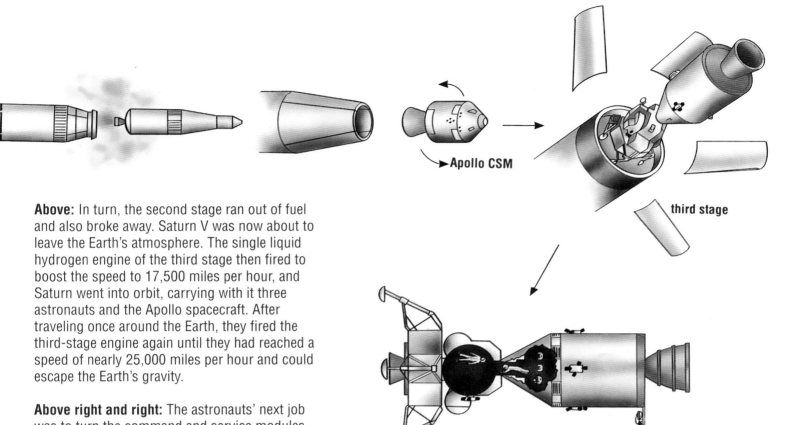

Above: In turn, the second stage ran out of fuel and also broke away. Saturn V was now about to leave the Earth's atmosphere. The single liquid hydrogen engine of the third stage then fired to boost the speed to 17,500 miles per hour, and Saturn went into orbit, carrying with it three astronauts and the Apollo spacecraft. After traveling once around the Earth, they fired the third-stage engine again until they had reached a speed of nearly 25,000 miles per hour and could escape the Earth's gravity.

Above right and right: The astronauts' next job was to turn the command and service modules (CSM) and dock with the lunar module, pulling it clear of the third stage. They were now in the correct configuration for their three-day journey to the Moon.

Apollo CSM

third stage

lunar module

CSM

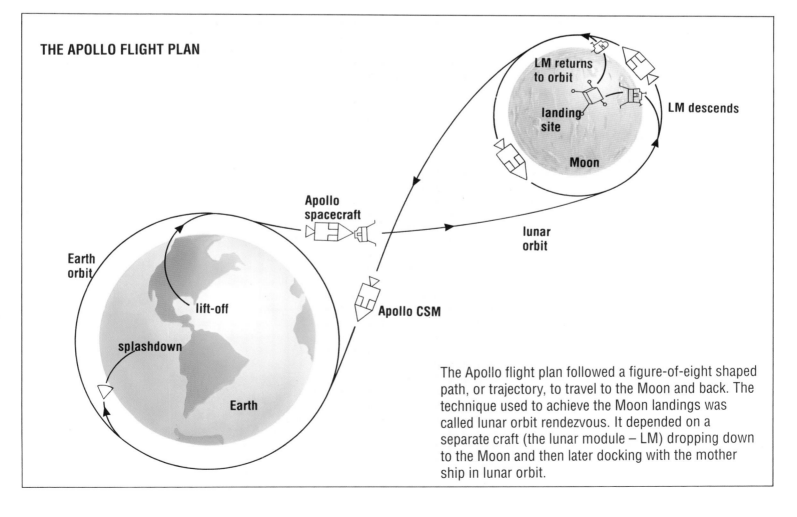

THE APOLLO FLIGHT PLAN

LM returns to orbit

landing site

LM descends

Moon

lunar orbit

Apollo spacecraft

Earth orbit

lift-off

Apollo CSM

splashdown

Earth

The Apollo flight plan followed a figure-of-eight shaped path, or trajectory, to travel to the Moon and back. The technique used to achieve the Moon landings was called lunar orbit rendezvous. It depended on a separate craft (the lunar module – LM) dropping down to the Moon and then later docking with the mother ship in lunar orbit.

THE LUNAR SURFACE

When Neil Armstrong stepped down on to the surface of the Moon on July 20, 1969, he said: "That's one small step for man, one giant leap for mankind." Edwin Aldrin soon took his first steps. These astronauts, from Apollo 11, were followed over the next few years by five other two-astronaut teams from Apollos 12, 14, 15, 16, and 17. The last left the Moon in December, 1972.

Apollo 11 landed in one of the lunar seas, the Sea of Tranquility. Apollo 12 landed in the Ocean of Storms. The other crews landed in more rugged, highland regions. From the samples the astronauts brought back and the photographs they took, we now know almost as much about the Moon's surface as we do about the Earth's!

Almost everywhere the surface is covered with a loose, dusty soil and scattered rocks. There are craters, large and small, all over. They were made by lumps of rock raining down from outer space.

The rocks that make up the lunar seas are typically dark and heavy. They are much like the volcanic rocks on Earth we call basalt. The typical rocks of the highland regions are lighter in weight and color. Many rocks are made up of little chips

Below: A lunar landing site. The lunar module stands on a desolate, but strangely beautiful landscape. The surface is covered with a thick layer of dust. It is pitted with craters, and strewn with rocks. The horizon is closer than it is on Earth because the Moon is so much smaller.

cemented together. They are like a rock we have on Earth, called breccia. Most of the minerals found in the Moon rocks are similar to the minerals found in the rocks on Earth.

The lunar astronauts carried out a number of experiments and also set up groups of instruments that radioed their readings back to Earth. These included seismometers, which are instruments that record tremors in the ground. On Earth, they record earthquakes; on the Moon, they recorded moonquakes. From moonquake measurements scientists have figured out what the interior of the Moon is like.

Above: Apollo 17 astronaut Harrison Schmitt gets down to some lunar "gardening" He is actually carrying out tests on the lunar soil. He was the last of the astronauts to leave the Moon, on 14 December 1972.

THE PLANETS

The Earth and eight other large bodies circle around the Sun and at different distances from it. These are the bodies we call the planets. The word planet means "wanderer." The ancient astronomers gave them this name because they looked like stars that wandered across the celestial sphere. The proper stars always stayed in fixed positions (see page 8).

The ancients were familiar with five of the planets – Mercury, Venus, Mars, Jupiter, and Saturn – because they are visible to the naked eye. Mercury is quite difficult to see, but the others often shine brilliantly. They shine, not because of their own light, but because they reflect light from the Sun, a star. Only stars give off their own light. The three outermost planets were discovered comparatively recently: Uranus in 1781, Neptune in 1846, and Pluto not until 1930.

There are great differences among the planets. Earth belongs to a group of inner planets, which circle relatively close to the Sun. They are as different from the outer planets as chalk from cheese.

The inner planets are relatively small rocky balls, like the Earth, and they are often called the terrestrial (Earth-like) planets. They contrast markedly with the four outer planets Jupiter, Saturn, Uranus, and Neptune. These planets are giant balls of gas and liquid gas. They probably do not have any solid surfaces.

Space probes have revolutionized the study of both the inner and outer planets in recent years. These have flown past or landed on the planets and sent back detailed pictures and information. Only Pluto has not yet been visited. It is so remote that it still remains as mysterious a body as ever.

The nine planets in our solar system travel around the Sun in more or less circular orbits (**main picture**). The four small rocky planets, Mercury, Venus, Earth and Mars, lie quite close together. The other planets are separated by vast distances. The outermost planet, Pluto, takes nearly 250 years to circle once around the Sun. There is a great difference in size between the inner and outer planets (see **inset**). King of the planets, Jupiter, could swallow up 27,000 bodies the size of Mercury!

Planet	Average distance from Sun (millions miles)	Diameter at equator (miles)	Circles Sun in
Mercury	36	3,015	88 days
Venus	67	7,545	225 days
Earth	93	7,926	365.25 days
Mars	142	4,220	687 days
Jupiter	484	88,600	11.9 years
Saturn	887	75,000	29.5 years
Uranus	1,783	32,500	84 years
Neptune	2,794	31,000	165 years
Pluto	3,670	1,440	248 years

KEY

1 Sun	6 Jupiter
2 Mercury	7 Saturn
3 Venus	8 Uranus
4 Earth	9 Neptune
5 Mars	10 Pluto

METEORS AND COMETS

The planets were formed about 4,600 million years ago, when great swarms of ice-covered bits of rock came together. However, there were many icy bits of rock left over. They are still around today. A large collection of lumps ended up circling the Sun in a broad band, or belt, between the orbits of Mars and Jupiter. We call them the asteroids, or minor planets. Even the biggest, called Ceres, is no more than 625 miles across.

Not all the asteroids stay within the asteroid belt. Some have orbits that take them much nearer the Sun. A few wander rather too close to Earth for comfort. In March, 1989, one passed within 500,000 miles. This may not seem close, but in celestial terms it was a very near miss!

However, some rocky bits from outer space hit us all the time. Fortunately, they are mostly very small. They shoot into the Earth's atmosphere at high speed, and friction with the air makes them glow white-hot and burn up to dust. From the Earth we see them as fiery streaks, which make it appear as if the stars are falling. We call these streaks meteors. Sometimes bigger lumps bombard the Earth and survive to reach the ground. We call them meteorites.

We see other wandering icy lumps of rock as comets. For most of their lives, these lumps remain invisible. Only when they get near the Sun do they start to shine, like "hairy stars." That was one of the names the early astronomers gave to comets. Most comets appear suddenly. But a few return to our skies regularly. Halley's comet – the most famous comet of all, returns every 75/6 years. We last saw it from Earth in 1986.

Above: Some 25,000 years ago a huge lump of rock from outer space smashed into the Earth and created this huge crater, in what is now the Arizona Desert. It was a meteorite, with a mass of perhaps a quarter of a million tons. The Arizona Meteor Crater measures about 4,150 feet across and 570 feet deep.

Left: Halley's comet was last seen from the Earth in 1986. This picture was taken in the spring, when it was heading away from the Sun and back into the depths of the solar system. It was then travelling tail-first. The tail of a comet always points away from the Sun. The solar wind creates the tail by "blowing" dust away from the body of the comet.

Left: The asteroids (see arrow) circle in a broad band between the orbits of Mars and Jupiter. Some astronomers once thought that they were the remains of another planet.

MERCURY AND VENUS

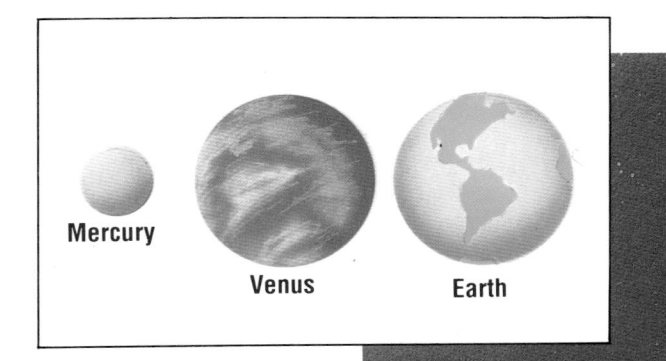

Mercury

Venus

Earth

Above: Mercury and Venus compared to the Earth. Venus (diameter 7,500 miles) is a near twin of the Earth; Mercury (diameter 2,950 miles) is much smaller.

Right: The Moon and Venus in the evening sky. At times, Venus shines so brilliantly it has even been known to cast shadows.

Right: The heavily cratered surface of Mercury, pictured by the Mariner 10 space probe in 1973.

Two planets circle closer to the Sun than the Earth does. Mercury is closest. It is a ball of rock, baked by the Sun, and with temperatures of 842°F or more. It is about half as big again as the Moon. Mercury looks something like the Moon, too. Its whole surface is smothered in craters. But unlike the Moon, it does not have any large areas of plains or seas.

Mercury stays very close to the Sun in the sky and is therefore difficult to see from Earth. The next planet out, Venus, could not be more easy to spot. We see it as the evening star, shining brilliantly in the west as the Sun goes down. Apart from the Moon, it is the brightest object in the night sky.

Venus is much easier to see than Mercury for several reasons. One, it is much bigger – nearly as big as the Earth. Two, it is much nearer. And three, it is always covered in white clouds, which reflect the Sun's light brilliantly.

The atmosphere of Venus is a lot thicker than that of the Earth. At the surface the atmospheric pressure is nearly 100 times that on Earth. The main gas in the atmosphere is carbon dioxide. The clouds are made up of droplets of sulphuric acid. The thick atmosphere lets the energy from the Sun through, but then traps it, something like a greenhouse does. Because of this "greenhouse effect," the temperature on Venus is 842°F or more. This is hot enough to melt lead.

Underneath Venus's permanent clouds, the surface appears to consist of rolling plains with two main highland areas, or continents. They are Aphrodite Terra, which is about the size of Africa, and Ishtar Terra, about the size of Australia.

PLANET EARTH

Left: The Earth, photographed by astronauts traveling in orbit around the Moon, during the first Apollo landing mission in July 1969. The blue of the oceans, the brown of the continents and the white swirls of cloud are clearly visible. How different the planet looks from the drab, waterless Moon.

Right: A false-color picture of Death Valley in California, one of the hottest and driest places on Earth. It was taken by a Landsat satellite. Pictures taken from satellites reveal a fascinating variety of landscapes on Earth. They show mountains, deserts, rivers and volcanoes, and provide evidence of human habitation – roads and bridges, fields and cities.

Right: Elephants quenching their thirst at a waterhole in Africa. Water holds the key to the Earth's most unique feature – life. Living things can exist without food for quite long periods, but without water they soon die.

Earth is a planet, just like Mercury, Venus, and the others. It is a ball of rock that circles in space around the Sun and spins on its axis as it does so. All planets do this. But the Earth is unique among the planets in one very important way – it is able to support life.

For life as we know it to thrive, four main things are needed: carbon compounds, water, oxygen, and temperatures that are not too hot nor too cold. Only Earth provides the right combination of these things.

There are plenty of carbon compounds and water – more than two-thirds of the Earth's surface is water. The Earth's atmosphere provides the oxygen for living things to breathe. It also acts as a blanket to prevent too much of the Sun's heat from escaping back into space at night.

The atmosphere has another function too. It has a layer of ozone (a kind of oxygen), which filters out ultraviolet rays coming from the Sun. In very large doses these rays would be harmful to life. There are signs that air pollution on Earth is starting to destroy the ozone layer. This must be prevented at all costs if we, and other life on Earth, are to continue living the way we do.

Another major difference between Earth and its neighbors in space is that it has a very young surface, which is changing all the time. The Earth changes because of activity above and below the ground. Much of the change is brought about by the weather. In time, the action of wind, rain, heat, and frost will reduce even high mountains to dust.

Under the top, hard crust of the Earth, the rocks are still partly molten. This causes the continents to drift, volcanoes to erupt, and earthquakes to occur. In general, Earth's neighbors have a surface that has changed little for millions of years.

MARS

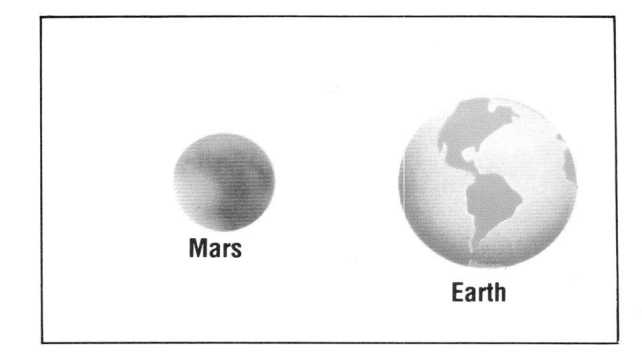

Above: Mars compared in size with the Earth. It has a diameter of 4,200 miles, just over half that of the Earth.

Below: A Viking space probe took this picture of Mars as it approached the planet in 1976. The great gash in the surface is the 3,000 mile long Mariner Valley.

The Romans named the planet Mars after their god of war because its reddish-orange color reminded them of the fires and destruction wars cause. When its two small moons were discovered (1877), they were named Phobos ("fear") and Deimos ("terror") after the horses that pulled Mars's chariot. The reddish color of Mars certainly makes it stand out in the night sky, which is why we often call it the Red Planet.

Because Mars is a neighbor in space, people used to wonder whether it could support any life. But we now

know that it almost certainly cannot. Space probes have shown it to be a very cold, nearly airless planet, with no signs of intelligent Martians, or indeed of life of any kind. Two Viking probes have landed on Mars and tested the soil for life, but could not find any.

The pictures sent back by space probes have revealed a very varied landscape on Mars. Some regions are a crater-strewn wilderness of canyons and deserts. One great canyon, called Mariner Valley, runs for nearly 3,000 miles. In another region, there is a

huge ridge topped by three massive volcanoes. Nearby is an even bigger volcano named Olympus Mons, some 15 miles high: the biggest volcano in the solar system.

At the poles, ice caps grow in the winter. They are made up mainly of water ice, showing that there is some water on Mars. But none flows in rivers as it does on Earth. A little is present in the very thin atmosphere, and clouds sometimes form there. There are dark surface markings which change from season to season. These are caused by dust storms.

Above: A Viking lander on Mars. Two spacecraft like this landed in different regions, called Chryse and Utopia. The photographs they sent back showed a very similar landscape in both regions. There is loose soil and scattered rocks, rusty red in color. The sky is pinkish-orange.

JUPITER

Left: Jupiter in comparison to the Earth. It has a diameter of 88,700 miles, eleven times that of the Earth. But it is still dwarfed by the Sun, which is nearly ten times as big.

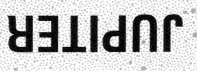

Earth

Jupiter

The Romans considered Jupiter to be king of their gods, and it is an appropriate name for the king of the planets. Jupiter is enormous, and is big enough to swallow over one thousand Earths. In fact, it has more than twice the mass of all the other planets put together.

Jupiter shines brightly in the night sky on many nights of the year even though it is so far away. One reason for this is because it is covered with clouds. Through a telescope, we can see that the clouds form multicolored bands parallel to the planet's equator.

Among the bands there are all kinds of whirls and white and red spots. The largest, called the Great Red Spot, is larger than the Earth. Close-up photographs taken by space probes have shown that the Great Red Spot is a huge storm; it has been raging for centuries.

Jupiter is quite different from the rocky Earth-like planets. Its very deep cloudy atmosphere is made up mainly of hydrogen gas. Underneath there is not a solid surface, but a vast deep ocean of hydrogen in a liquid state. Only at the very center of the huge planet might there be a ball of rock.

Like the other giant planets, Jupiter has many moons circling around it – at least 16. Four of them are so big that we can see them with binoculars. The biggest, called Ganymede, is even bigger than the planet Mercury!

Left: Jupiter, shown in a montage with its four largest Moons. They are not drawn to scale. The Moons are Io (far left), noted for its erupting volcanoes; Ganymede (second left), the largest moon; smooth, icy Europa (top); and dark, heavily-cratered Callisto.

Right: Jupiter's most distinctive feature is the Great Red Spot, a huge storm center, about 17,500 miles across.

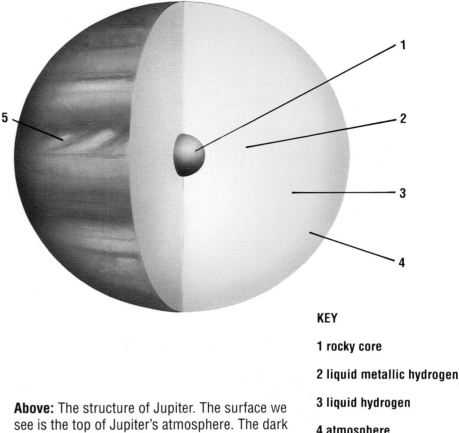

Above: The structure of Jupiter. The surface we see is the top of Jupiter's atmosphere. The dark bands (belts) and the light bands (zones) are formed by clouds, drawn out by the planet's rapid rotation.

KEY

1 rocky core

2 liquid metallic hydrogen

3 liquid hydrogen

4 atmosphere

5 clouds

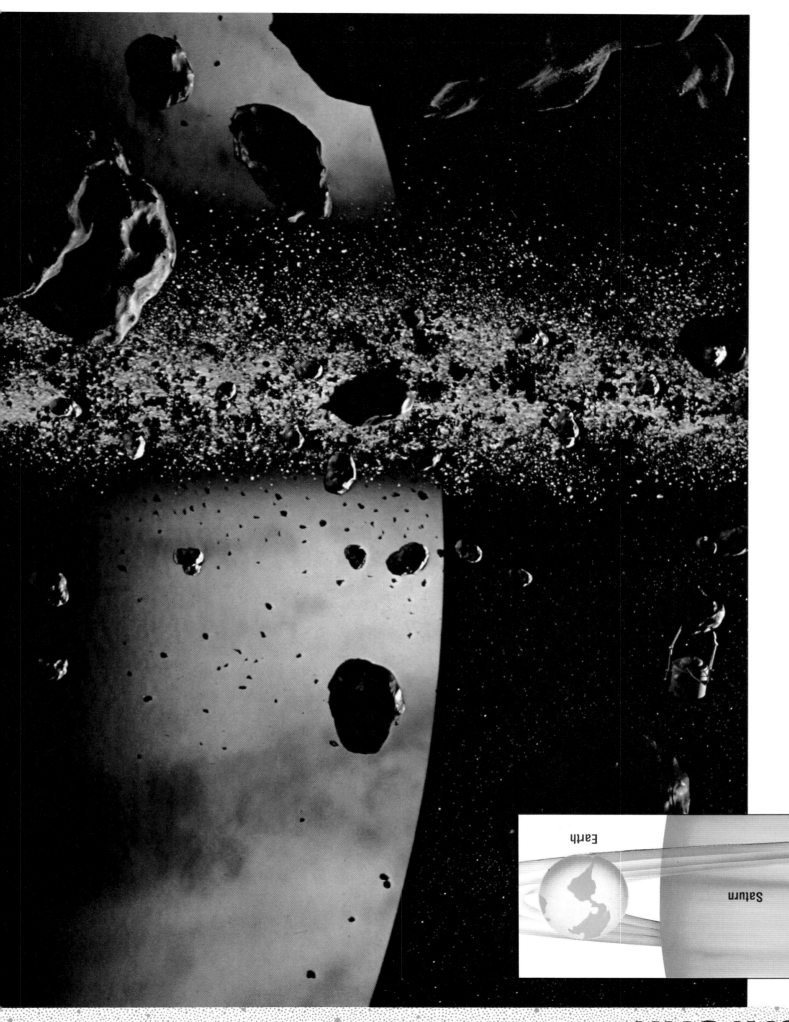

SATURN

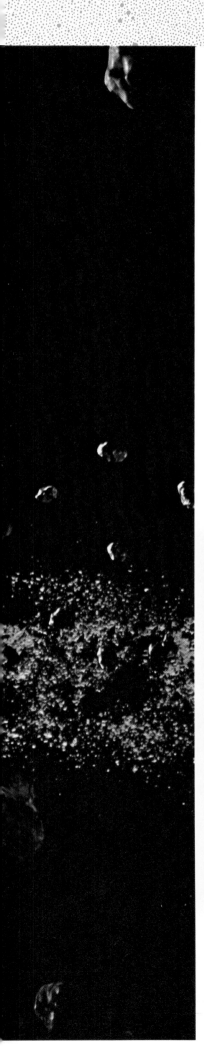

aturn, the next planet out beyond Jupiter, is the most beautiful planet of all. This is because it is encircled by a system of bright shining rings. We now know that the other giant planets have faint ring systems, but they are no match for Saturn's.

Saturn is the second largest planet after Jupiter, and it resembles Jupiter in some respects. It is made up mainly of hydrogen gas and liquid hydrogen. But it is not as dense as Jupiter. In fact, if you could place it in water, it would float!

Like Jupiter, Saturn has parallel bands of clouds in its atmosphere. But they are not as prominent as Jupiter's cloud bands. The clouds are forced into this parallel pattern by violent winds blowing in the atmosphere. In places these winds reach a speed of more than 1,100 miles an hour.

THE GLORIOUS RINGS

From the Earth we can see three rings girdling Saturn's equator. They are broad but thin. Some years we see the rings edge-on, and they almost disappear from view. In places they are only about 650 feet thick.

Space probes have shown that there are many other rings around Saturn, too faint to be seen from Earth. These rings are, in fact, made up of thousands of separate ringlets. Each one is made up of lumps of rock of different sizes, which circle the planet at high speed. The lumps appear to be kept in place by the gravitational pull of tiny moons nearby, which have been called shepherds.

Left: A close-up view of Saturn's glorious ring system. It is made up of millions of chunks of rock of various sizes, traveling swiftly in orbit around the planet. With a diameter of 75,100 miles, Saturn is nearly ten times the size of the Earth (**see inset**).

Above: A Voyager space probe took this picture of Saturn and its rings. The inner part of the ring system is so transparent that we can see through it. The two outer rings are the brightest. They are separated by a dark gap, called the Cassini division, after the astronomer who first noted it.

URANUS

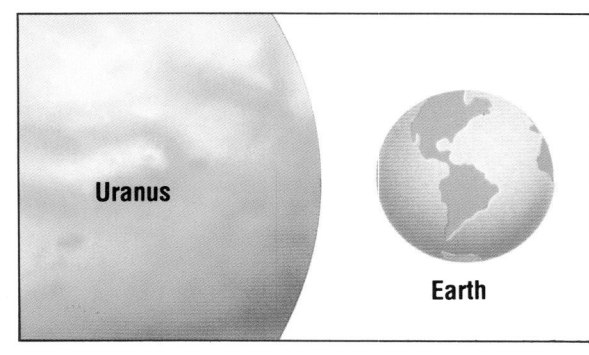

Above: Uranus compared in size with the Earth. It has a diameter of 32,000 miles, about four times that of the Earth.

Below: Uranus and its system of faint rings travel through space sideways because of the planet's tilted axis.

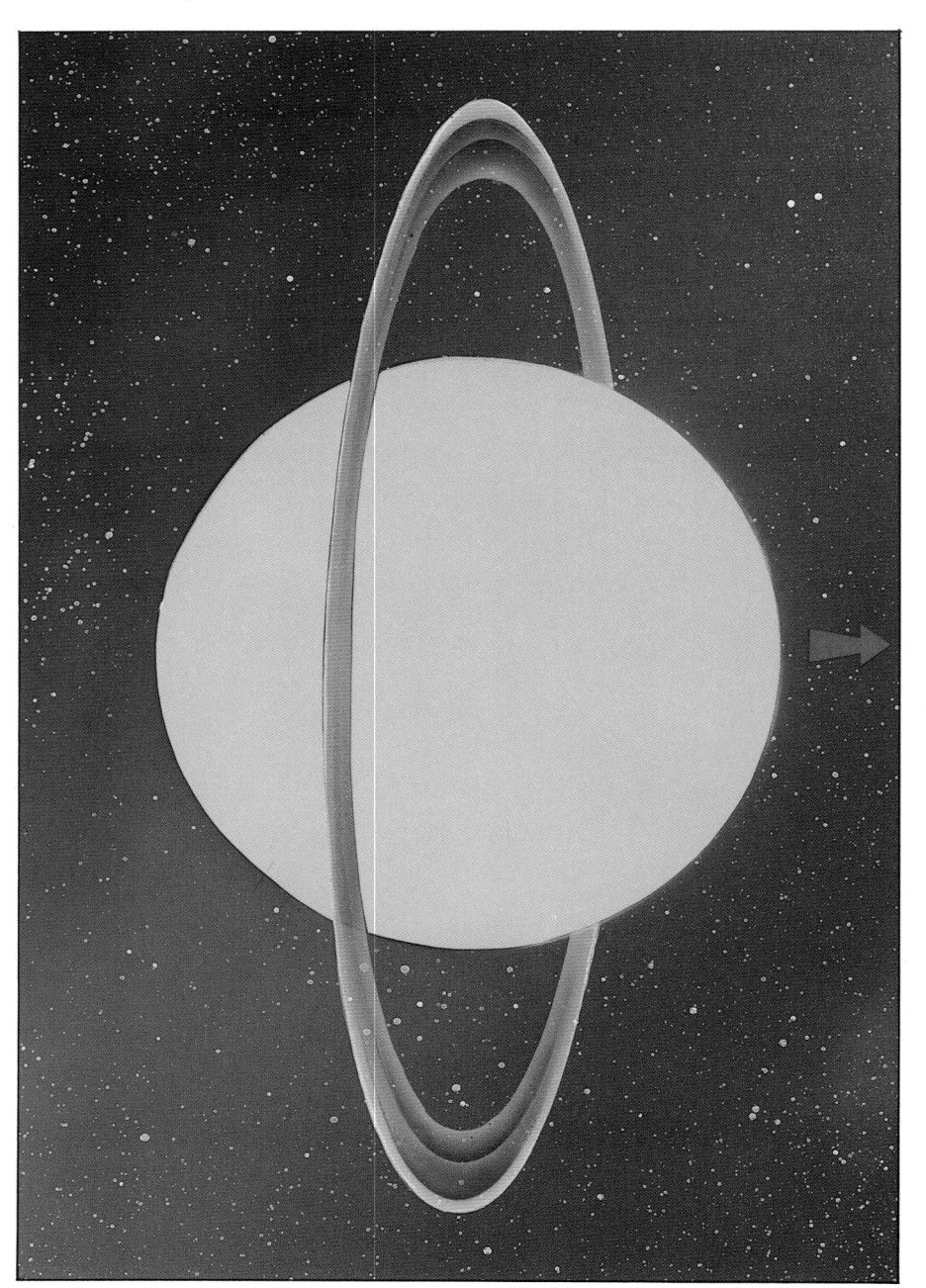

Uranus lies twice as far away as Saturn, and is too far away for us to see with the naked eye. The English astronomer William Herschel was the first person to train a telescope on the planet in 1781. To begin with he thought it was a comet, but soon realized it must be a planet from the way it was moving.

Uranus is so far away that it takes 84 years to circle around the Sun. It revolves on its axis like the other planets, but in a peculiar way. It spins on its side as it travels. The other planets spin in a nearly upright position, like a top.

THE HOT WATER OCEAN

Uranus is the third largest planet. It has a different make-up from Saturn and Jupiter. Above a central core of molten rock and metal, there is a deep hot ocean of water and ammonia. On top of this, there is a deep atmosphere, made up mainly of hydrogen and helium. Traces of methane are also present. This gas absorbs red light, which leaves the planet looking a greenish-blue. A few clouds can occasionally be seen in the atmosphere.

About 15 moons circle around Uranus, but only the five biggest can be seen from Earth. The most interesting of these by far is Miranda. Photographs taken by the Voyager 2 space probe show it to have the most fantastic landscape. Astronomers think this might have been caused when the moon was once shattered to pieces but then came together again.

Right: This is what Uranus would look like from its moon, Miranda. Miranda is a rocky body about 190 miles across. Unlike the other giant planets, Uranus seems rather featureless. There are no signs of cloud banding or of stormy areas.

Left: Neptune compared with the Earth and Pluto. It is slightly smaller than Uranus, with a diameter of about 30,000 miles. Pluto is tiny, only about 1,400 miles across.

NEPTUNE AND PLUTO

After the discovery of Uranus, astronomers found that its path through space was not as it should have been. So they guessed that yet another planet, even farther out, was affecting Uranus by its gravity.

After 65 years, in 1846, that planet was discovered by the German astronomer Johann Galle. It was named Neptune. Neptune is almost a twin of Uranus in size, being only a fraction smaller. Little can be seen of it from Earth, even with the most powerful telescopes because it lies so far away.

Neptune was almost a complete mystery until it was visited by the Voyager 2 space probe in 1989. Pictures show it to be colored deep blue. Clouds scurry through its atmosphere, which also shows dark spots. These are thought to be storm centers, something like Jupiter's

Great Red Spot. Voyager also revealed that Neptune has a faint ring system, like Uranus and Jupiter. It also discovered several new moons.

PLUTO

We know hardly anything about Pluto, except that it is by far the smallest planet and must be a deep-frozen world. One interesting thing we do know is that it has a moon half its size. Pluto is the most recent planet to be found, in 1930 by the astronomer Clyde Tombaugh. It is so small and so remote that even the most powerful telescopes show it only as a star-like point of light.

For most of the 248 years it takes to orbit the Sun, Pluto is the most distant planet. Since 1979, however, it has been traveling inside Neptune's orbit. Not until 1999 will it regain its rightful position as the most distant planet.

Above: An artist's impression of Pluto and its large moon Charon. Charon has a captured rotation, circling Pluto in six days, the same time it takes Pluto to rotate once on its own axis.

Far left: In the pictures sent back by the Voyager 2 probe, Neptune is a glorious blue color. Puffs of white cloud appear in the atmosphere, together with dark spots where storms are brewing.

SPACE VOYAGERS

On August 20, 1977, a powerful Titan rocket launched a probe into space on the most ambitious journey of the Space Age. The probe was Voyager 2, and its momentous mission was to rendezvous with four of the outer planets.

The space scientists who designed the probe were taking advantage of an alignment of the planets that would not be repeated for almost two centuries. Their planning was meticulous, and their spacecraft flawless. In turn, Voyager visited Jupiter (July, 1979) and Saturn (August, 1981). Ingeniously, it used the enormous gravity of these gas giants to speed it up and fling it in the right direction, for the next fly past, of Uranus, in January, 1986.

From Uranus, Voyager sped on to Neptune. It arrived there on August 24, 1989, exactly on time. By then it had traveled almost 4,500 million miles. When it sent back radio signals from Neptune, it took them over four hours to reach the Earth.

Astonishingly, the quality of the pictures radioed back was excellent. Now Voyager is heading out of the solar system. Early in the next century it will leave the system behind and start an endless journey through interstellar space. It will be following the deep-space trail blazed by the Pioneer 10 probe, which in 1983 became the first spacecraft to journey out of the solar system towards the stars.

Voyager could, in about 30,000 years time, draw near to Sirius, the brightest star in the heavens. But maybe it will not get that far. Maybe it will be found by intelligent creatures on another planet, near another Sun, somewhere in the uncharted depths of our Galaxy . . .

When Voyager 2 flew past Neptune in 1989, it was over 4,000 million miles from Earth. It had set out from that remote planet 12 years earlier, visiting Jupiter, Saturn and Uranus on the way. After traveling so far and for so long, it arrived at Neptune within minutes of its scheduled time!

KEY

1 Sun	2 Mercury
3 Venus	4 Earth
5 Mars	6 Asteroid belt
7 Jupiter	8 Saturn
9 Uranus	10 Neptune
11 Pluto	

VOYAGER 2

A Dish antenna
B RTG nuclear generator
C Magnetometer boom
D Electronics boxes
E Calibration panel
F Science instruments boom
G Cosmic-ray detector
H TV cameras
I Radiation detector

OTHER WORLDS

Above: Somewhere out in space, many light-years from Earth, an alien civilization may be setting out from its home planet. Their centuries-long voyage of exploration. Their mission is to find a planet like their own in another solar system. Their own planet is under threat because their sun is about to die.

A re there other planets circling around other Suns somewhere out there in space? And do they hold intelligent life like ourselves, or indeed life of any kind?

Most astronomers would answer: "Almost certainly yes," to both these questions. They would point out that there are millions of stars in our Galaxy alone that are like the Sun. Many must have planets circling around them with conditions similar to those on Earth.

On at least some of these planets,

the kinds of processes that produced life on Earth must have taken place. So some forms of life must have developed. It is not known if these extraterrestrial ("outside the Earth") lifeforms will be like those that exist on our planet.

Only if we visit them, or they visit us, will we be able to find out. Probably we will communicate first by radio. The trouble is that a radio message between our two worlds could take hundreds, maybe thousands, of years to make a one-

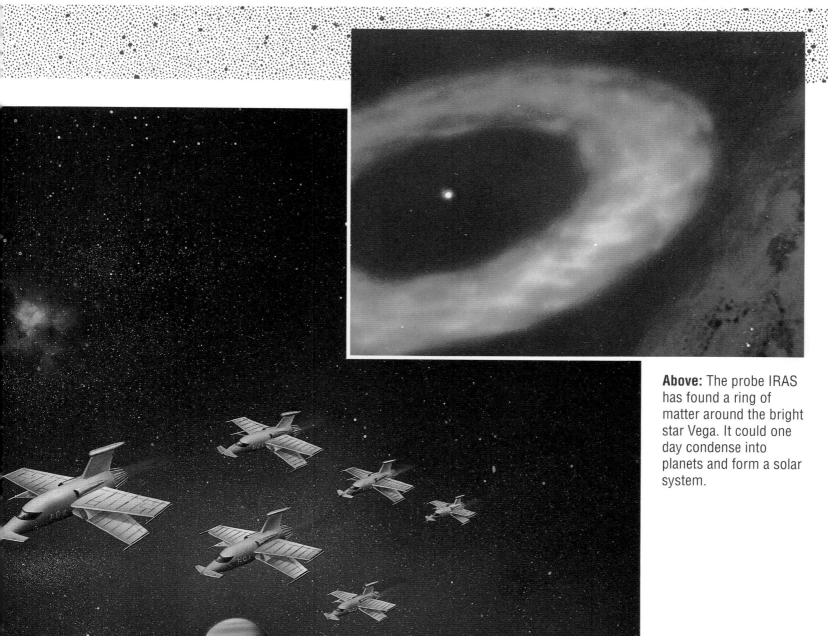

Above: The probe IRAS has found a ring of matter around the bright star Vega. It could one day condense into planets and form a solar system.

way journey. This would make conversations rather difficult, even if we could speak the same language!

Many people are convinced that beings from other worlds have already visited the Earth. They say they have seen alien spacecraft, and even talked with alien creatures. Certainly many strange objects have been reported in the skies over the years. We call them UFOs, meaning unidentified flying objects.

Usually UFOs turn out to be such things as weather balloons, high-flying aircraft, and even unusual forms of lightning. But a few sightings are unexplained, and so a doubt remains.

Possibly, just possibly, these UFOs could be interstellar reconnaissance craft seeking a hospitable planet for an alien lifeform. Perhaps this alien civilization lives on a planet about to be engulfed by a star that is soon to enter its red-giant stage. Perhaps they have found that Earth is just what they are looking for and are already on their way toward us. Perhaps, perhaps. What do you think?

INDEX

Figures in **bold** refer to captions

A

air pollution 63
aircraft, high-flying 77
Aldrin, Edwin 52, 54
Algol (Winking demon) 22
alien spacecraft **76**, 77
ammonia 70
Andromeda galaxy 32, 34, 36
Aphrodite Terra 61
Apollo 11 52, 64
Apollo 12 54
Apollo 14 54
Apollo 15 54
Apollo 16 54
Apollo 17 54, **55**
Apollo Moonlanding Project **52**
Apollo space missions 49, **52**, **53**, 54, **62**
Arecibo, Puerto Rico 38, **39**
Aristotle 8
Arizona Meteor Crater **59**
Armstrong, Neil 52, 54
asteroids 58, **59**
astrology 8
astronauts 41, 52, **52**, **53**, 54, **55**
astronomers 4–5, 6
    and asteroids **59**
    and comets 58
    and eclipses 46, **46**
    and extraterrestrial lifeforms 76
    and galaxies 34, **34**, 38
    and the Moon 49
    and origin of the universe 12, **12**, 13
    and the planets 56, **59**
    and satellites 15
    and the stars 9, 10, **14**, 18, **28**
    and telescopes **4**, **14**, 17, 38
    and Uranus 70, 73
atmosphere
    Earth's 52, 58, 61
    and electromagnetic waves 15
    Jupiter's 67, **67**
    and Mars 65
    and Neptune 73, **73**
    and positioning of observatories 17
    Saturn's 69
    of stars 18
    and Uranus 70
    Venus's 61
atoms **12**, 42
Auriga **19**
aurora 42–3
Aurora Australis **42**
Aurora Borealis **42**

B

Babylonia 8
Bangka Island **46**, 47
Barred-spiral galaxies 34
basalt 54
Betelgeuse 18
Bible 12
Big Bang **12**, 13
Big Crunch 13
Big Dipper constellation 23, **23**
binary stars 22, **22**
binoculars **4**, 16, 49, **49**, 67
black holes **28**, 29
Brazil 47
breccia 55

C

calcium 18
Callisto **67**
cameras, telescopes as **14**, 17

Canes Venatici **23**
canyons (on Mars) 65
Capella **19**
captive rotation 50
carbon compounds 63
carbon dioxide 61
Cassini division **69**
celestial latitude **9**
celestial longitude **9**
celestial poles **10**
celestial sphere 8–9, **9**, 56
Centaur constellation 23
Centaurus A galaxy 36, **36**, 38
Ceres 58
Chaldea 8
Charon **73**
chemical elements
    in stars 15
    in the Sun 18
Chryse (Mars) 65
clouds
    on Jupiter 67, **67**
    on Mars 65
    on Neptune 73, **73**
    on Saturn 69
    on Uranus 70
    on Venus 61
clouds (nebula) 24, 26, **27**
clusters, star **19**, 22–3, 33, 36
    globular 23
    open 23, **23**
Coal Sack 24
comets 4, 58, **59**
computers, and telescopes **15**, **39**
constellations 10–11, **10**, 22, 24, 32
    see also under individual constellations
continents
    Earth 63
    Venus 61
corona 41, **45**, 46, 47
craters
    on Earth **59**
    on Mars 65
    on Mercury **60**, 61
    on Moon **49**, 54, **54**
Creation 12
Crux (Southern Cross) **19**
CSM (command service module) 52, **53**
Cygnus **29**

D

dark nebulae 24
Death Valley, California **62**
debris 58
declination **9**
Deimos 64
distances in space 6, **32**, **56**
double stars 22, **22**
dust
    in atmosphere 17
    and Centaurus A 36
    and comets 58
    and galaxies **25**, 33, **36**
    and nebulae 24, **24**, 26, **27**, **29**
    storms 65
    and the Sun 30

E

Earth 57, **59**, **62**, **75**
    and alien lifeforms 77
    atmosphere of 52, 63
    creation of 12
    and death of Sun, 30, **30**
    early life on 30

    effect of atmosphere on rays 15
    measurement on 6
    orbit around the Sun 18, 19, 41, 45, **50**, **56**
    position in the universe 6, **7**, 8
    shadow of 45
    shape of 8
    size of **60**, **64**, **66**, **69**, **70**, **72**
    and solar wind 42, 43
    spinning on axis 9, 41, 63
    surface changes 63
    water on **62**, 63
earthquakes 30, 55, 63
eclipse
    of binary stars 22, **22**
    lunar 45, **45**
    partial solar 45
    total solar 45, **45**, **46**, **47**
ecliptic **9**
Effelsberg, Germany 38
Egypt 8
electromagnetic waves 15
elliptical galaxies 34
energy
    and Big Bang 13
    given out by stars **14**, 15, **24**, **26**
    and star birth **12**, 27
    of Sun 41, 42
    and supernova 28
Europa **67**
"evening star" 4, 61
extraterrestrial lifeforms 76, 77
eyes, and viewing stars 16

F

film, photographic 17
Finland 47
Full Moon 59

G

galaxies 6, 12, **12**, 15, 32, **32**
    barred-spiral 34, **34**
    and clusters 36
    elliptical 34, **34**, 38
    interacting **37**
    irregular 36
    radio 38
    spiral 34, **34**, **35**
    Toadstool 36, **37**
Galaxy 6, **7**, **25**, 32, **32**, 33, 34, 36, **39**, 74, 76
Galle, Johann 73
gamma rays, and stars 15
Ganymede 67, **67**
gas
    and galaxies 33
    and nebulae 24, 26
    and planets 56
    and Sun 30, 41
globular clusters 23
gravity
    and black holes **28**, 29
    and Earth 51, 52
    and Moon 51
    and planets 74
    and Saturn's moon 69
    and star birth **12**, 26
    and star death 28, **28**
Great Nebula, Orion **27**
Great Red Spot 67, **67**, 73
greenhouse effect 61

H

"hairy stars" 58

Halley's comet 58, **59**
Hawaii 47
heat (from Sun) 30, 41, 42
Heaven 12
helium
    and stars **26**, 27
    and Sun 18
    Uranus 70
Herschel, William 70
Hertzsprung-Russell diagram **20**
horoscopes 8
Horsehead Nebula **24**
Hubble, Edwin 12, 34, **34**
hydrogen
    and Jupiter 67
    and nebulae 24
    and stars **12**, **26**, 27, 28, **37**
    and Sun 18
    and Uranus 70

I

infrared rays, and stars **14**, 15, **27**
instruments, astronomical 5, 15, **15**, 18, **75**
intelligent life 74, 76
interstellar matter 24
interstellar space 74
Io **67**
IRAS satellite **14**, **27**, 77
iron 18
irregular galaxies 36
Isaac Newton telescope **16**
Ishtar Terra 61

J

Jacobus Kapteyn telescope **15**
Jewel Box star cluster **19**
Jupiter 56, **56**, **57**, 58, **59**, **66**, 67, **67**, 69, 70, 73, 74, **75**

K

Kapteyn, Jacobus, **15**
Kennedy, President John F. **52**
Kennedy Space Center 52
Kitt Peak observatory **17**

L

Landsat satellite **62**
Large Magellanic Cloud 36
life, dependence on Sun 30
light
    and Galaxy 33
    from stars 6, **7**, **14**, 15, 16
    from Sun, **7**, 30, 41, 42
    and telescopes 16
light-years 6, **32**, 36
lightning 77
liquid gas, and planets 56
liquid hydrogen 69
Local group 36
lunar craters **49**
lunar eclipse 45
lunar module (LM) **53**, **54**
lunar orbit rendezvous **53**
Lyra constellation 24

M

M3 cluster **23**
Magellan, Ferdinand 36
magnesium 18
magnetic storm 43
magnitudes of brightness 20
Mariner 10 space probe **60**
Mariner Valley 65

Mars 56, **56**, **57**, 58, **59**, 64–5, **64**, **65**, **75**
matter
    and Big Bang 13
    interstellar 24
    and stars 24, **77**
Mayall reflector **17**
Mercury 30, **56**, **57**, **60**, 61, 67, **75**
meteorites 58, **59**
meteors 58
methane 70
Mexico 47
microwaves, and stars 15
Middle East 8, 10
Milky Way Galaxy **10**, **19**, **27**, 32, 34
    see also Galaxy
Miranda 70, **70**
mirrors, and telescopes **15**, 16–17, **16**, **17**
Mizar 22
Moon 4, 6, **60**, **62**
    distance from earth 49
    full 50
    gravity of 51
    interior of 55
    lack of life 49
    landings on 49, 52, **53**, 54
    light of 49
    and lunar eclipse 45
    orbit round Earth 45, 50, **50**
    phases 50, **51**
    rocks on 54–5, **54**
    seas 49, **49**, 54
    shadow 45
    size of 49, **54**
    and solar eclipse 45, **46**, **47**
    spinning on axis 50, **50**
moonquakes 55
moons
    and Jupiter **67**
    and Neptune 73
    and Pluto 73, **73**
    and Uranus 70, **70**
Mt Wilson Observatory, California 34

N

nebulae 24
    dark 24
    planetary 24
    and star birth 26
    see also under individual nebulae
Neptune 56, **57**, **72**, 73, **73**, 74, **75**
neutrons 29
night sky 10
Northern Hemisphere **10**, 36, 42
Northern Lights 42, **42**, **43**
nuclear fusion 27, 28, 41

O

observatories **14**, **15**, **16**, 17, **17**, **38**
Ocean of Storms 54
oceans
    and tides 51
    and Uranus 70
Olympus Mons 65
Omega Centauri 23
open clusters 23
optical doubles **22**
Orion 18, **24**, **27**
oxygen 63
ozone 63

P

parallax **18**, 19

Parkes radio observatory **38**
partial solar eclipse 45
path of totality 45
patterns, star
    see constellations
Perseus constellation 22
Peru 47
philosophers 8, 12
Phobos 64
photographs, and telescopes 17
    of Jupiter 67
    of Moon 54
    of stars **9**, 14
photosphere 41
planetary nebulae 24
planets 4
    alignment of 74
    differences among 56
    discovery of 56
    formation of 58
    and lifeforms 76
    minor 58
    sizes of 56
    and solar system 41, **56**
    spinning on axes 70
    terrestrial 56
Pleiades cluster 23
Pluto, 56, **56**, **57**, **72**, 73, **73**, **75**
Polaris **10**
Pole star **9**, **10**
priest-astronomers 8, 10
prominences 41, **41**, 46, 47
protons 42
Proxima Centauri 6, 20
pulsars 29

Q

quasars **38**, 39

R

radiation **41**, 42, **75**
    and nebulae 24
    and stars 15, **27**
radio astronomy 38–9
radio communications 43
radio galaxies 38
radio pulses 29
radio signals **14**, **39**, 74, 76–7
radio waves, and stars **14**, 15, 29, 38–9, **38**, 42, 43
red giant stars 28, **28**, 77
Red Planet see Mars
reflectors **15**, 16–17, **17**
refractors 16, **17**
right ascension **9**
Ring nebula 24
ring systems 69, **69**, **70**, 73
rocks
    Earth's 63
    and Mars **56**, **65**
    and Mercury **56**
    and Moon 54–5
    and planets 58
    and Saturn's rings 69, **69**
    and Uranus 70
    and Venus **56**
Romans 64, 67
Roque de los Muchachos **15**, **16**

S

Sagittarius **25**
Sagittarius A **39**
satellites, astronomical **14**, 15, **27**, **62**

Saturn 56, **57**, 69, **69**, 70, 74, **75**
Saturn V rocket 52, **52**, **53**
Schmitt, Harrison **55**
Sea of Tranquility 54
seas, and Moon 49, **49**, **50**
seismometers 55
Semirodniki, Mt 17
Seven Sisters 23
shepherds 69
Sirius 20, 74
Skylab **41**
Small Magellanic Cloud 36
solar eclipse 45, **45**, **46**, **47**
solar system, 6, **6**, 41, 49, **56**, **59**, **76**, **77**
solar winds 42–3, **59**
South Atlantic 47
Southern Cross constellation **19**, 24
Southern Hemisphere **10**, 23, **23**, 36, 42–3
Southern Lights **42**, 43
space 4
    and Big Bang 13
    electromagnetic waves in 15
    scale of 6
space probes 56, 65, 69, **69**, **73**, **77**
spacecraft 52, **65**, 74
    alien **76**, **77**
Spacelab **43**
spectroscope 18
spectrum **19**
    examining lines of 18
    spectral classes 20
spiral galaxies 34, **34**, **35**
star clouds **25**
stars
    binary 22, **22**
    birth of 26–7, **27**
    blue giant **23**
    brightness of 18, **19**, 20, **20**, **22**, 74
    chemical elements in 15, 18
    clusters **19**, 22–3, **23**, 33
    cool **19**, 20
    death of 26, 28–9, **28**
    double 22, **22**
    eclipse of 22, **22**
    energy from 15
    fixed 8, **9**, 10, 56
    in Galaxy 33
    hot **19**, 20, **23**
    life dependent on mass 27
    light from 6, **9**, **14**, 15, 16, 18
    measuring distances 18–19, **18**, 20
    movement of **9**, 10, 15, 18
    nearest 6, 20, **20**
    photographing **14**, 17
    pinpointing positions of 9, **9**
    red giant 28
    size of 18
    and spectrum 18, **19**, 20
    supergiant 18, 28, **29**
    supernova 28, **29**
    temperature of 15, 18, **19**
    viewing 16, 17, **18**
    white dwarf 28, 29
sulphuric acid 61
Sun 6, **7**, **32**, **42**, **57**, **75**, 76
    brightness of 18, **41**
    chemical elements in 18, 41
    death of 30, **30**
    dependence of living things on 30, 41
    Earth's orbit around 19
    gravity 41
    life of 27, **28**

    light of **7**, 49, 61
    lone travel through space 22
    and Mercury 61
    planets circling around 56, **56**
    as red giant 28, **28**, **30**
    rising and setting of 9, 41
    size of 28, 41, **66**
    and solar wind 42–3
    surface of 41, **41**
    temperature 41, 63
    and Venus 61
    as white dwarf 28
sunspots 41, 43
supergiant stars 18, 28, **28**
supernova 28, **29**

T

Taurus constellation 23
telescopes **4**, 5, **16**, 22, 24, 32, 47, **49**, 67, 70, 73
    as giant cameras **14**, 17
    radio **14**, 38, **38**, **39**
    reflector **15**, 16–17, **17**, 34, 38
    refractor 16, **17**
    and satellites 15
tides **50**, 51, **51**
time, and Big Bang 13
Titan rocket 74
Toadstool galaxies 36, **37**
Tombaugh, Clyde 73
total solar eclipse 45, **45**, 46–7, **46**, **47**

U

UFOs (unidentified flying objects) 77, **77**
ultraviolet rays, and stars 15, 63
universe 4, 5, 39
    expansion of 12, **12**, 13
    and Galaxy 33
    origin of 12, **12**
    position of Earth in **6**, 8
    size of 6
Uranus 56, **57**, 70, **70**, **72**, 74, **75**
Utopia (Mars) 65

V

Vega **77**
Veil Nebula **29**
Venus 4, 30, 56, **56**, **57**, **60**, 61, **75**
Viking probes **64**, 65, **65**
Virgo constellation **35**
volcanoes 30, **62**, 63, **64**, 65, **67**
Voyager 2 space probe 70, 73, **73**, 74, **75**

W

water
    on Earth **62**, 63
    on Mars 65
    and Uranus 70
wavelengths 15, 18
weather balloons 77
white dwarf stars 28, **28**, 29
winds
    on Saturn 69
    solar 42–3
Winking demon (Algol) 22

X

X-rays, and stars 15, 42

Y

year, and Earth's orbit of Sun 41
yellow dwarf 18

ACKNOWLEDGMENTS

Front cover illustration and pages 66–7 by Paul Doherty

Other illustrations by Oxford Illustrators:
Simon Lindo, Jonathan Soffe, Andrew Reeves, Howard Twiner, Stephen Hawkins, Ray Webb.

All photographs supplied by **Robin Kerrod** with the exception of the following pages:
Octopus Picture Library 51 (**Mike Busselles**), 59 top, 63 bottom.
David A. Hardy/Science Photo Library 73